CRITICAL ✺
✺ THINKING
— IN THE —
ELEMENTARY ✺
CLASSROOM

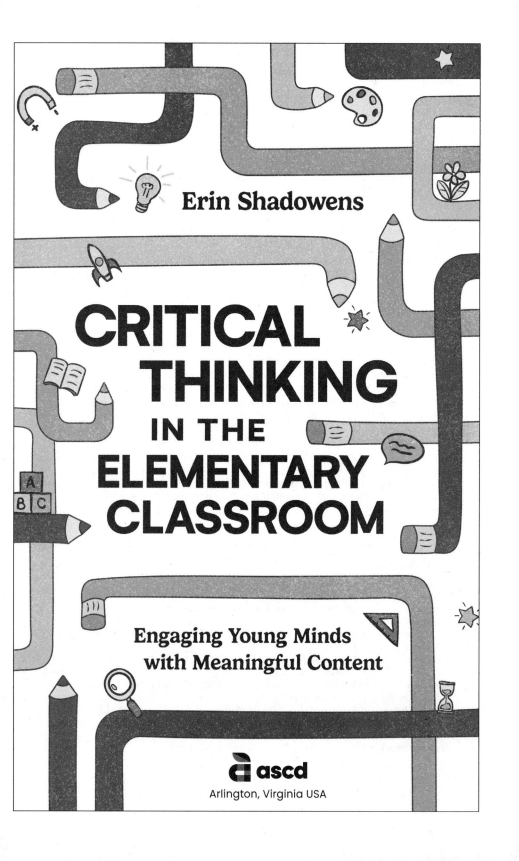

Erin Shadowens

CRITICAL THINKING
IN THE
ELEMENTARY
CLASSROOM

**Engaging Young Minds
with Meaningful Content**

ascd

Arlington, Virginia USA

2800 Shirlington Road, Suite 1001 • Arlington, VA 22206 USA
Phone: 800-933-2723 or 703-578-9600 • Fax: 703-575-5400
Website: www.ascd.org • Email: member@ascd.org
Author guidelines: www.ascd.org/write

Richard Culatta, *Chief Executive Officer;* Anthony Rebora, *Chief Content Officer;* Genny Ostertag, *Managing Director, Book Acquisitions & Editing;* Susan Hills, *Senior Acquisitions Editor;* Mary Beth Nielsen, *Director, Book Editing;* Jennifer L. Morgan, *Editor;* Thomas Lytle, *Creative Director;* Donald Ely, *Art Director;* Melissa Johnston/The Hatcher Group, *Graphic Designer;* Valerie Younkin, *Senior Production Designer;* Kelly Marshall, *Production Manager;* Shajuan Martin, *E-Publishing Specialist;* Christopher Logan, *Senior Production Specialist*

PAPERBACK ISBN: 978-1-4166-3243-6   ASCD product #123012 n10/23

PDF EBOOK ISBN: 978-1-4166-3244-3; see Books in Print for other formats.

Quantity discounts are available: email programteam@ascd.org or call 800-933-2723, ext. 5773, or 703-575-5773. For desk copies, go to www.ascd.org/deskcopy.

Library of Congress Cataloging-in-Publication Data
Names: Shadowens, Erin, author.
Title: Critical thinking in the elementary classroom : engaging young minds with meaningful content / Erin Shadowens.
Description: Arlington, Virginia USA : ASCD, [2024] | Includes bibliographical references and index.
Identifiers: LCCN 2023022899 (print) | LCCN 2023022900 (ebook) | ISBN 9781416632436 (paperback) | ISBN 9781416632443 (pdf)
Subjects: LCSH: Critical thinking—Study and teaching (Elementary) | Problem solving—Study and teaching (Elementary)
Classification: LCC LB1590.3 .S4153 2024 (print) | LCC LB1590.3 (ebook) | DDC 370.15/2—dc23/eng/20230606
LC record available at https://lccn.loc.gov/2023022899
LC ebook record available at https://lccn.loc.gov/2023022900

33 32 31 30 29 28 27 26 25 24   1 2 3 4 5 6 7 8 9 10 11 12

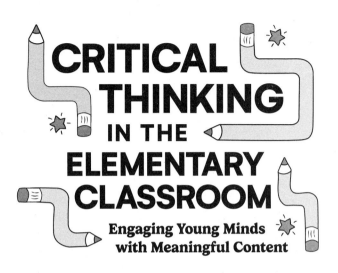

CRITICAL THINKING IN THE ELEMENTARY CLASSROOM

Engaging Young Minds with Meaningful Content

INTRODUCTION

In 2010, the National Governors Association and the Council of Chief State School Officers finalized and released the Common Core State Standards—a breakdown of grade-level learning expectations in English language arts (ELA) and math for grades K–12. Many states rapidly moved to adopt these standards, seeking to raise the achievement of all students across the United States.

These sets of standards appeared in an environment concerned with developing "21st century skills." Incorporated in the mission statements of countless educational institutions, the term *21st century skills* suggests a change from education's status quo, implying that the evolution of technology and industry in the new millennium demands an updated vision for what and how students learn in school. When we search "21st century skills" online, the first few results link to webpages listing skills such as critical thinking, creativity, collaboration, and problem solving—and critical thinking nearly always tops the list.

Popular arguments for the Common Core standards still resonate today. Proponents appreciate their nationwide consistency and clear guidance for schools and teachers. Yet their rollout championed an even more compelling argument: that the shift to these standards would set America's children on a path toward the grand prize of education—they would learn not only *what* to

1

think but *how* to think; through mastery of the standards, they could become critical thinkers (*Los Angeles Daily News,* 2017). While no one in education, including the Common Core developers, ever purported to find a panacea for all of the field's ills, the standards certainly inspired a great deal of optimism. Teachers reported seeing a shift in the depth of thinking in their class, even when they struggled with the new standards (An & Cardona, 2019).

Behind most comprehensive projects to improve education, such as the Common Core, are two aims: raise overall achievement and foster critical thinking in young people. The latter aim tends to overwhelm the first. Many—philosophers, politicians, principals, teachers, parents, community members—identify the ability to think critically as the ultimate objective of an education. Stakeholders hunger for a magical recipe with a few discrete ingredients that will lead to widespread, if not universal, critical thinking. The concept of critical thinking evokes a number of literary clichés—say, the Holy Grail or Melville's white whale—all with common characteristics: something fantastic but almost indefinable; hard-sought but elusive.

It's often easier to point out the absence of critical thinking than its presence. Consider one of the released questions from the 2018 international PISA assessment, taken by 15-year-olds around the world (Organisation for Economic Co-Operation and Development [OECD], 2019). Students first read the webpage of a business that sells dairy products, then an article from a health-focused website. The first article extolled the benefits of drinking cow milk, while the second article warned the reader that the benefits may be oversold if not incorrect.

PISA questions are ranked 1–6 based on their difficulty, with 1 representing the least difficult and 6 the most difficult. Based on students' responses, they are given a Level 1–6 score, which represents the types of questions they were able to answer. Level 1–3 questions may ask about the main idea and factual points in the article. As the levels increase, so does the question difficulty (OECD, 2016). A Level 5 question has students categorize statements from both texts as either "Fact" or "Opinion." What were some of the statements? "Drinking milk and other dairy products is the best way to lose weight," and "Several studies have questioned the bone-strengthening power of milk." The first clearly describes an opinion because it uses a subjective word like *best.*

The second statement states a fact about several studies but withholds any judgment on whether the studies are correct.

Only 13.5 percent of assessed students from the United States scored at a Level 5 or 6 in reading, the highest scores. A vast majority of test-takers struggled to answer questions like the fact and opinion ones described above.

What does this mean in practice? While it may not be necessary for many students to do well on the higher-difficulty questions, especially if the types of questions do not assess relevant knowledge or skills, the results should still give us pause. Individuals regularly consult information found from a wide variety of sources similar to the websites in the PISA questions. The ability to synthesize and critique that information matters, and it is concerning how many young people just a few years away from adulthood and voting struggle to do so. At a minimum, the inability to sort commonly encountered facts and opinions shows a decisive lack of critical thinking skills.

Since the widespread adoption of Common Core Standards more than a decade ago, the tenor of the standards discussion in the United States has changed, largely as a result of student performance on international and national standardized tests such as PISA and the National Assessment of Educational Progress (NAEP). The NAEP, known as "the Nation's Report Card," assesses 4th, 8th, and 12th graders across the country every two years. In 2019, approximately 600,000 students took the exam in English language arts and math. The NAEP results that year painted a bleak picture of student performance about a year before the COVID-19 pandemic caused lockdowns and major disruptions to the learning experiences of millions. Between 1992 and 2009, test scores in reading and math rose steadily; however, since 2009, test scores in reading and math have either stagnated or dipped. Math scores at the 25th percentile have particularly declined (Loveless, 2022), which means that the lowest performing students are falling further and further behind their peers. The most recent release of NAEP scores from spring 2022 showed the most severe decline in the performance of 9-year-olds since 1990 (NAEP, n.d.). For proponents of the Common Core, the correlation of underwhelming NAEP scores and the adoption of new standards is unsettling. While it would be easy to point fingers at school closures and remote learning, the downward trends predated the COVID-19 pandemic.

The question of how to develop critical thinkers is as pressing as ever. In fact, the concerns about critical thinking are arguably more pronounced today than they were two decades ago. Political polarization and the proliferation of news sources have led to concerns about misinformation, media literacy, and the degradation of civic discourse. So how can educators address critical thinking in schools and classrooms? Despite a decades-long effort to raise the achievement of all students and innumerable articles bemoaning the state of American education, claiming there is a simple response to the question seems foolhardy. In a world where American schools do not equitably teach reading and math, we are left wondering if it is even possible to develop critical thinking in school.

Those two words—*critical* and *thinking*—can lead us astray. *Critical* comprises many meanings, such as critique, deconstruction, analysis. The term *critical* leads some to think of critical thinking in the negative, as if it only works to pull things apart rather than put them together. In fact, both of these meanings matter a great deal. The word *thinking* can also mislead. *Thinking* acts as both a noun and a verb. It implies that thinking is one single thing— both a process and state of being, an entity that either is or is not *critical.*

But critical thinking is not one, or even a set of, stand-alone processes. What we call critical thinking is an emergent property of building knowledge and expertise. *The Stanford Encyclopedia of Philosophy* likens an emergent property to a tornado, which emerges from complex interactions among dust, debris, and cold fronts. The tornado becomes its own entity, both distinct from and dependent on all its parts (O'Connor, 2021). Much of what we call critical thinking similarly depends on the interaction of many elements.

To create the conditions where critical thinking can emerge, elementary educators need a mindset shift. Too often, assumptions about the capacities of young students act as barriers. Some educators use the terms *developmentally inappropriate* and *too advanced* to dismiss introducing students to rich novels, science, history, geography, and complex tasks at a young age. Standards are more often used as the ceiling for what students can do rather than the floor. This mindset wrings out everything that may be fascinating and challenging about a topic. In the words of my student, who was describing a science video designed for young children, "They dumb everything down for kids to the point where you don't even learn anything interesting."

If we want to improve outcomes for our students, and if we want to see more kids engaged in what we call "critical thinking," we have to start here: *expand our definition of possible.*

We must expand our definition of possible for the minds and intellectual lives of students in elementary school. This does not mean boring, mind-numbing learning experiences where teachers deliver lectures to students strapped to desks. It means opportunities for students to build knowledge across different subjects, grapple with interesting questions, and take on new challenges. Rather than dumb down what students learn, we need to level up instruction.

To engage in critical thinking, our students need real challenges and supportive learning environments that make those challenges accessible. The world is full of complexity, yet so often curricula for young children drain all the juicy idiosyncrasies and smooth out the finicky wrinkles that make learning an exhilarating experience. Some teachers outright skip standards or teach below-grade-level content. In the name of rigor, some schools batter young children with dull texts and tasks that are supposed to yield 21st century career-ready adults, but instead, they ossify the learning process. But introducing challenge and complexity should not condemn students to boredom. Rigor doesn't mean constructing unsolvable mazes with our questions, rubrics, and exemplars. We shouldn't give kids something hard for the sake of hardness. Our challenges to students must be purposeful tasks by which they can learn, grow, and thrive.

Moreover, expanding our definition of possible applies not just to students identified as advanced or gifted. Even teachers with the best of intentions sometimes reduce their expectations due to the deficits they perceive in children. Teachers sometimes think they are supporting children when they are actually creating additional barriers. When we expand our definition of possible, we do it for *all children*—even if they receive special education services, even if they qualify for free or and reduced-price lunch, even if they experience challenges in their home life, even if they struggle with behavior, even if there are a litany of factors telling us to write someone off. Our job as educators is to see the glowing possibilities in the children we work with.

We teachers need to believe from the outset in the capacity of children to learn—especially now. Two years of disrupted schooling during the pandemic demonstrated how too many institutions put children's well-being aside. Our students deserve a vehement recommitment from adults to their potential.

This book is for educators—teachers, grade teams, instructional coaches, administrators—who want to raise the bar for their students. While engaging with the book, I ask readers to bring an ethos of open-mindedness as well as a critical eye. Most of the chapters describe integrated thinking processes that occur simultaneously in a teacher's preparation and instruction. As you read the chapters, think of the practices you already have in place in your class-rooms and schools and consider ways to refine and adapt them. Some of the practices and ideas in this book may be entirely new to you and may even con-flict with information you have previously learned in a teacher preparation program or professional development session. Explore these new practices with an open mind. I encourage interested readers to research the references and further reading recommendations at the end of the chapters.

Chapter 1 focuses on defining critical thinking. A discussion of critical thinking cannot get off the ground without a working definition. I discuss common misunderstandings associated with critical thinking while explor-ing research into expertise and knowledge building in literacy.

Chapter 2 introduces the Critical Thinking Framework. The framework breaks down how teachers can nurture deeper thinking in the context of content-focused lessons. This chapter also includes three case studies to demonstrate what the framework looks like when implemented. It ends with a K–5 continuum describing how the framework progresses throughout ele-mentary school.

Chapter 3 turns to creating and implementing an ambitious vision for academic achievement. I discuss the importance of investing in high-quality curriculum, analyzing student work exemplars, and preparing instruction that builds subject knowledge expertise.

Chapter 4 digs deeper into how the Critical Thinking Framework comes alive at the lesson and unit levels. I walk readers through common instructional pitfalls and offer specific suggestions for structuring lessons for deep thinking and processing.

Chapters 5 and 6 work in tandem to discuss the relationship between assessment and feedback. Assessment and feedback are the most powerful tools for revealing and nurturing student thinking, working together to create a virtuous cycle that propels academic achievement and deep thinking.

Chapter 7 steps away from academics to discuss the significance of school and classroom culture. The classroom environment needs the same meticulous attention as any curriculum or lesson plan. Teachers and school leaders need to build culture with intention, such as habits of risk taking and intellectual honesty. I discuss specific ways teachers can create and sustain a community where kids can take on challenges in and beyond the classroom.

I am a true idealist about children's capacity to think. I have learned, often the hard way, how difficult it is for teachers to create the environment required for rich conversations and deep thinking. For a long time, I assumed the ideals were the problem. Yet I now know execution matters as much, if not more, than the ideals themselves. We can make our classrooms a better world than the one beyond its four walls, but we need to focus on *how* we get there. It requires careful planning, patient execution, and a stomach for failure. The nitty-gritty details make or break what's possible.

This book is, above all else, about the *craft* of teaching. Throughout all these chapters, I aim to provide readers with practical knowledge that can be implemented with real students. I offer principles flexible enough to work in a variety of settings. This is not a book of platitudes; every chapter focuses on the nuts and bolts of instruction, particularly the type of instruction that supports the development of critical thinking. The work is complex, and it requires us to critically reflect on the practices currently used in our schools and districts. There are also no shortcuts—no computer program or scripted curriculum can do more than supplement the thoughtful planning of educators.

As we move forward, let us remember we are expanding the definition of possible not only for children but also for elementary educators. The work of elementary teachers matters, and this book will never apologize for taking the minds of young children and the adults who teach them seriously. As John Steinbeck (2002) says in his essay "... Like Captured Fireflies," teaching "might even be the greatest of the arts since the medium is the human mind and spirit" (p. 142). The minds and spirits of young children, to borrow Steinbeck's phrase, are a precious responsibility. The foundation children receive in the early grades sets the stage for later life. Teachers must engage in the necessary intellectual preparation to meet the demands of that responsibility. This book aspires to contribute to that preparation.

When we prepare for the unique rigors of teaching, we honor the special role we play in children's lives. Let's embark together, never forgetting the challenge, beauty, and thrill contained in our important work.

1 WHAT DO WE MEAN BY CRITICAL THINKING?

Critical thinking is a thorny term. We certainly seem to know when critical thinking is *not* present, like when a student confuses facts and opinions about the benefits of cow's milk, as in the PISA question described in the Introduction. It's a term schools and newspaper columnists throw around frequently, yet it is so ill-defined and vague that no one is certain about its definition. Is critical thinking identifiable but not describable—we only know it when we see it?

There have been efforts to define critical thinking. The American Philosophical Association attempted to write a definition almost three decades ago in *The Delphi Report*. Unlike most dictionary definitions, *The Delphi Report's* is a substantial paragraph, beginning with critical thinking as "self-regulatory judgment" and then listing a variety of dispositions particular to critical thinking, such as "habitually inquisitive," "open-minded," and "honest in facing personal biases" (Facione, 1990, p. 2). This definition has informed a number of studies on the subject, including a 2015 meta-analysis (Abrami et al., 2015). Echoing *The Delphi Report*, cognitive scientist Daniel Willingham (2007) proposed a three-part definition of critical thinking where the thinking is novel (not a regurgitation of memorized facts), self-directed, and effective. Others argue for a more inclusive definition of critical thinking that is as interested in justice in present social issues as it is in principles of logic.

All of these good-faith efforts to define and explain critical thinking can help teachers better understand its characteristics. Unfortunately, however, teachers and administrators work in a time-poor context, and the plethora of prevailing ideas around critical thinking can seem quite complicated. Most of us struggle to meet the demands of the job in a typical workday, and we only have so much time dedicated periodically to professional learning.

Debates over the definition of *critical thinking* more often obfuscate than clarify what we mean by the term, especially for teachers. Depending on the source, critical thinking can be abstract logic or ineffable creativity or a general disposition of criticality. The pedagogical implications are even less clear. Should schools explicitly teach certain universal tenets of critical thinking or step back and allow children to discover their problem-solving abilities through authentic environmental experiences? Despite bold declarations from different camps, no broad consensus exists. Observers of these debates can fairly ask if there are *any* reputable ways to develop critical thinking in a classroom setting. Everyone seems to agree critical thinking is relevant to the lives of learners, whether in preparation for the voting booth or for the important personal and career decisions every adult faces. But for educators, the issue isn't whether critical thinking is important, but whether the teaching of critical thinking is practical and actionable within the context of schools and classrooms.

For this reason, I prefer the definition found in the *Oxford English Dictionary*: critical thinking is "the objective, systematic, and rational analysis and evaluation of factual evidence in order to form a judgment" (n.d.).

The nouns here are helpful—*analysis, evaluation, judgment*—especially when we transform them into verbs. We want students to analyze the world around them, evaluate information and arguments for quality and credibility, and judge, or make decisions, based on their analysis and evaluations—such as forming opinions or making important choices, from the academic to the ethical, financial, and political.

A definition is a starting place, but definitions do not create units or lesson plans, and a definition certainly does not inculcate sound analysis, evaluation, and judgment in learners. For the rest of this chapter, we are going to turn our attention to how these crucial features manifest in the learning process by considering the wealth of research into how learners learn to think about complex topics. We will look at studies into how expertise and expert thinking progress in different domains, as well as studies into the role of knowledge in literacy. As we will see, both children and adults struggle to analyze, evaluate, and judge without the prerequisite knowledge to engage in complex thinking.

Before we proceed, I want to address a point of contention. The majority of research important to our understanding of critical thinking in the classroom uses quantitative measures. A fair objection is that quantitative measurements fail to fully capture how imagination, emotional intelligence, and socially subversive lines of thought contribute to critical thinking. In truth, there is no study or meta-analysis that provides a standardized way to say, "Look, that's a curriculum that helps students question the status quo *and* improve test scores." But there shouldn't have to be. We can care about children's ability both to master academic content and to develop a wider criticality about the world they inhabit. Both are essential aims for democratic citizens. For the first, we can look at scientific research for evidence-supported practices. The second is harder to quantify and, therefore, difficult to research. We will look closely at the second toward the end of the book, though we will frequently see opportunities for critical consciousness in the effective classroom practices discussed throughout the book.

Prerequisites for Critical Thinking

What does it mean to *know* something? The question, not out of place in a Platonic dialogue or a David Lynch dream sequence, has been investigated by philosophers and scientists alike for millennia. It at first doesn't seem like a particularly interesting question to ask, especially since most people think the answer is obvious: "You either know something or you don't." Yet the role of knowledge in learning is contested. Popular education materials and books encourage educators to focus on helping students "learn how to learn" and to hone metacognitive approaches to achieve success in the fast-paced 21st century economy (Building Learning Power, n.d.). Curriculum driven to cultivate learners rather than knowers will, in this formulation, lead to individuals who know both *how* to think and *when* to think effectively.

Personally, I am susceptible to these points. I spent my college years reading philosophy and engaging in freewheeling seminar conversations. My classmates and I were responsible for our own learning, and the ability to direct and attend to our own progress was crucial. And the learning-to-learn crowd has a point: a number of habits and soft skills are essential to the learning process, and educators should demystify them and teach them to students.

Yet little evidence undergirds the claims of learning-to-learn programs; rather, it is the ability to know about *particular* things that allows human beings to think effectively. Consider the following illustration:

> Harry usually chooses a kneading technique based on the hydration of his bread dough. He measures out 240 grams of warm water, 350 grams of flour, 9 grams of yeast, and 9 grams of salt. How should he go about kneading the bread?

Unless you are an avid bread baker, you may not know what hydration means, or how to calculate hydration, or why Harry alters his kneading style based on the hydration of the dough. Most experienced bread bakers, even if they do not use the jargon of hydration in their own baking, will realize the problem is asking them about the wetness of the dough. They will draw upon their knowledge and experience with different types of dough to decide how to move forward. The *thinking* required in this task depends on the *knowledge* of its components.

It would be fair to respond, "Of course you need to know something to think about it well, but you still need to be able to reason and to problem solve. Blind knowledge is also not critical thinking."

Over the last 60 years, cognitive scientists have studied the differences between novices and experts in order to better understand the nature of thinking. It will surprise no one that an expert in any field will surpass the novice in their ability to analyze, evaluate, and judge the problems and tasks within their fields. The question is, why are experts *so much better at thinking* than novices in their fields?

In a series of experiments in the '60s and '70s with novice and expert chess players, scientists showed the players quick images of midgame chessboards. The players were then asked to re-create the chessboards from memory. Higher-ranked players re-created these board formations with substantially more accuracy than lower-ranked players; in fact, the higher their rank, the more successful they were at the task. This finding alone is not significant. Someone might argue the experiment merely demonstrates that better chess players possess higher-capacity memories when compared with less successful players. Better memories equal better chess players. However, when all players were presented with random board configurations (i.e., configurations that were not possible in a chess game), all the players struggled to recall the visual representations (Frey & Adesman, 1976). These expert chess players could not recall random chess positions, only the ones resulting from a meaningful set of moves. This indicates that the highly ranked chess players' memories don't just have better storage capacity; rather, more game scenarios are stored in their memory than players with less expertise, which allows them to better recall and understand the game boards in front of them. They simply know more chess scenarios than novices do.

These experiments not only demonstrate a relationship between memory and expertise but also highlight the differences in how experts and novices think. In the Frey and Adesman study, researchers observed how the skilled chess players "not only identify more chunks and bigger chunks, but also discover more semantic relations among the pieces and among the chunks. This deeper level of processing may in fact be key to better retention" (p. 546). For these skilled players, recollecting game scenarios is intertwined with meaningful analysis. They are not just remembering—*they are thinking critically while they remember.*

Let's return to Harry the bread baker. Harry knows a lot about baking bread. He spends oodles of hours reading recipe books and baking blogs; he watches YouTube tutorials and PBS specials from the '80s. For years, Harry has experimented with hands-on baking to refine his technique. He even takes courses in his spare time. With this knowledge, Harry needs to decide how he should go about kneading his bread. He likes the ease of a mixer, but it is easy to overknead in a mixer, resulting in a tough dough. He can avoid that problem by hand kneading, but the cleanup is much trickier. Depending on the hydration of the dough, he might employ the French slapping technique to reduce stickiness or use a dough scraper. Harry activates his background knowledge to analyze his options, evaluate their efficacy, and judge the best course of action.

Now let's meet Phoebe. Phoebe does not know a lot about baking bread. She picked up a book about bread making because she thought it would be fun. Phoebe does not think about the hydration of the dough, so she does not think about whether the kneading technique suggested in the recipe book is the most efficacious. She attempts to imitate the pictures and written directions as best she can. Phoebe is overwhelmed by the directions and struggles to follow all the steps in the process. She is not analyzing, evaluating, or judging at all. She's just trying to get through it.

We see analogous scenarios play out in classrooms all the time. Some students look and sound like the skilled chess players and Harry the bread baker, but quite a few students share more in common with Phoebe, blindly and ineffectively following the recipe.

To understand the differences between experts and novices, we need to understand working memory and long-term memory. Working memory is the mind's capacity to think about something in the moment. It is extremely limited. Long-term memory refers to the brain's nearly limitless capacity for the storage of knowledge. The more domain-specific knowledge stored in long-term memory, like that of Harry the baker or a chess master, the less working memory is overwhelmed when presented with a new task within the domain (Sweller, 2016).

Psychologists call the mind's knowledge organization structure in long-term memory *schemata*, or *schema* in the singular. The mind, however, is not an organic encyclopedia with neatly alphabetized and ordered information. Far from it. The late psychologist David Rumelhart (1981) likened schemata to "theories of reality." Based on past experiences—such as immediate environments, books, media, and instruction—individuals develop theories about various aspects of their world that they then apply to new experiences. Throughout our lives, we are gaining and refining schemata, which is a much more complicated way of saying *we are always learning*. Much like a family tree that shows the branches and connections of an extended family, schemata are connected networks of associated information. When we learn something new, we incorporate it into what we already know about related topics, much like adding new leaves and branches to the image of a tree.

Consider the concept of *spring*. *Spring* contains within it associations with the season, the months of March through June, the unpredictable ebb between warm and cool temperatures, various religious and cultural holidays, even the notions of birth and renewal. For a classical musician, *spring* evokes the composers Vivaldi and Stravinsky, who set to music distinct visions of the word. But in another context, rather than the period between the vernal equinox and summer solstice, a *spring* is a coiled device, a key part of gag gifts and toasters. Physics professors have even more related information in their *spring* schemata, such as the ability to calculate elasticity via Hooke's law or to describe the concept of potential energy.

But these examples only address the noun *spring*. There is also the verb *spring*, which opens up a whole new web of connected ideas. *Spring* may indicate a type of jump or the bouncy way someone walks; idiomatically, someone who "springs into action" is a person who acts quickly.

Our *spring* schemata allow us to flexibly distinguish between these sentences:

"Oh, no," Fred gasped. "Dad says it's time for *spring* cleaning!"

The cricket *springs* from leaf to leaf.

The more someone knows about the permutations of a concept, the better they will be able to grasp its meaning in varying circumstances. "The knowledge embedded in our schemata forms the framework for our theories," writes Rumelhart (1981). "It is some configuration of these schemata which ultimately forms the basis for our understanding" (p. 18). The ability to understand and to think about a given topic hinges on knowledge.

Of course, not every schema is an accurate theory of reality. Misconceptions are often deeply rooted and difficult to revise. We'll talk more later in the book about teaching with misconceptions in mind.

The Transfer Problem

Critical thinking is not a discrete set of skills; rather, the ability to think critically emerges from increasing expertise in a specific domain. People can't analyze, evaluate, or critique without knowing something about the content they are analyzing, evaluating, and critiquing. A common misunderstanding is that critical thinking is an exclusive manner of thinking where particularly gifted individuals can transfer their "critical thinking skills" to every novel situation. This doesn't seem to be the case. In a meta-analysis reviewing interventions to support critical thinking, instruction embedded in content demonstrated higher effect sizes than contentless critical thinking approaches (Abrami et al., 2015).

Underpinning the problem with how critical thinking has been previously conceived is the idea of transfer. For example, some might claim, "If students learn general critical thinking skills or study a more 'general subject,' such as Latin or computer programming, they will be able to transfer their critical thinking skills to other areas." Nevertheless, minimal evidence supports broadly applicable critical thinking skills. As Daniel Willingham (2020) notes in *American Educator*, analysis, synthesis, and evaluation all mean different things in different disciplines.

One of the reasons transfer is difficult is because novices in a given field tend to be distracted by surface structures, which leads them to think through problems differently than experts. *Surface structure* refers to the most obvious elements of a problem or task. For instance, in math, students may notice the numbers in a word problem as well as the type of units (e.g., apples, brownies, marbles) and simply solve the problem based on how they solved another problem with similar superficial features. Most elementary school teachers experience this scenario almost every day: students will quickly add all of the numbers together and say, "Done!" I once had a student who said all math was adding numbers together, which is a decidedly superficial understanding of math problems. Without knowing the structures and principles of a given domain, novices cannot respond to tasks effectively.

Experts in a domain tend to approach problems by thinking about deep structures. They recognize consistent principles that undergird many types of problems and tasks, and they use those principles to respond more efficiently to novel scenarios. In a 2nd grade class, a student may notice, "This is one of those problems where it tells you how much you had at the beginning and how much you have at the end. Now I need to figure out the difference." As students gain expertise in a subject, they will notice certain regularities. However, the regularities in one subject do not necessarily transfer to another subject, which is why the school curriculum should equip students to learn about deep structures across many topics. The more subject-specific principles learned, the more flexible, and therefore critical, students can be in their thinking.

A Misleading Dichotomy: Procedural Versus Conceptual Knowledge

Some readers may experience cognitive dissonance after reading the previous section. Most teacher training programs emphasize the importance of higher-order thinking, often represented through Bloom's taxonomy (Bloom, 1956). In this model, knowledge of facts and procedures ranks far below demonstrations of understanding and creativity. We are led to believe we must climb a ladder, to use the metaphor embedded in the commonly shared visual of Bloom's taxonomy, to reach the top of the thinking pyramid. Benjamin Bloom himself did not intend the taxonomy to be seen this way. The lower tier of knowledge was a foundation on which the upper tiers were built. Yet educators tend to misinterpret Bloom's model by circumventing the lower tiers altogether. In service of critical thinking and student autonomy, many teachers will go straight to projects, inquiry, and complex application problems, treating factual knowledge as less essential than "higher levels of thinking." As a result, students never receive the foundation they need to do more complex thinking.

In schools, this conflict is typically reduced to the oversimplified battle between procedural and conceptual knowledge. Procedural knowledge represents the "memorization" side of the debate, characterized as students memorizing facts and procedures to the detriment of understanding the principles underpinning those facts and procedures. On the conceptual side, students are supposed to grasp the deeper "why" behind the ideas in a discipline, which tend to be more abstract and general. The procedural versus conceptual knowledge debate usually scapegoats procedural knowledge as the source of student misconceptions, asserting that if classrooms rebalance the scales to emphasize conceptual understanding, students will easily learn and employ procedures. The claim is that students need more time with concepts, full stop. Conceptual understanding will prevent the misunderstandings endemic to procedural learning.

Yet the distinction between procedural and conceptual knowledge is much more finicky than some imagine. One of the assumptions made by educators is that there is something fundamentally mindless or unthinking about procedural learning. When students are led to repetitively practice procedures, such as the standard algorithm for addition and subtraction, they are failing to think about what they are doing. On the other hand, critics argue, if students are thinking deeply about every step of the standard algorithm, they may also miss the bigger conceptual ideas in more advanced mathematics courses. A lack of procedural automaticity can undermine the development of conceptual understanding.

Educators need to move beyond seeing kinds of knowledge as antagonistic. Procedural and conceptual knowledge are better understood as partners in the learning process, not foes. Researchers Bethany Rittle-Johnson, Michael Schneider, and Jon R. Star (2015) describe the relationship between procedural and conceptual mathematics as "bidirectional." One type of knowledge does not necessarily outrank the other, nor should one type of understanding always precede the other in instruction. In their formulation, learning procedural knowledge reinforces conceptual knowledge and vice versa. They develop together, not in silos. This perspective is consistent with the research literature on reading instruction, which we will discuss later. (Quick preview: factual knowledge of vocabulary and language structures supports reading comprehension and understanding.)

Procedural and conceptual knowledge are not separate entities that can be taught without reference to the other. Much like a chemical reaction, the interaction between elements—in this case, procedural and conceptual knowledge—produces a new kind of understanding. Knowledge is transformative, not additive. Fluently reading a text at the speed of sight allows a reader to attend to the interesting ideas composed by the author; immediately recognizing the elements of the periodic table allows a chemist to think about the properties and composition of matter; a historian draws on a rich array of dates and events to contextualize a primary document. In all of these instances, and many more, procedural and conceptual understandings come together to yield deep analysis and evaluation of ideas, which is, by our definition, critical thinking.

Unfortunately, too many teachers in preparation programs and professional development sessions have only ever seen types of knowledge ranked into superior and inferior levels and tiers. What's the alternative? Rather than rank knowledge by tier, it is more fruitful to look at the depth of processing. How well information is retained differs based on how it is processed. Craik and Lockhart (1972) identify how information can be processed in a shallow or a deep way. Shallow processing is when the surface features of information are processed, like the appearance, spelling, or sound of that information. This is similar to a student trying to memorize the five boroughs of New York City by trying to remember how the words look, which is not so different from trying to recall a long list of meaningless symbols. It's incredibly difficult to remember something when you are focused only on superficial characteristics.

Deep processing connects new information to information you already know. The information is analyzed for meaningful throughlines. Rather than making a student try to remember New York City's boroughs by the appearance of letters in a long list, it is more powerful to make connections to other pieces of meaningful information, like where the boroughs are in relation to one another on a map. As cognitive scientist Daniel Willingham (2003) puts it, students remember what they think about. Knowledge that is processed in a shallow way, whether it is a procedural skill or a concept involving relationships of ideas, will likely not be retained in a meaningful way.

We will continue to talk about ways to elicit deep processing throughout the book. Deep processing is embedded in the Critical Thinking Framework (Chapter 2), the approach to instructional planning (Chapter 4), and recommendations for how to use assessment and feedback (Chapters 5 and 6).

Implications for Elementary School

What does this research about adult experts have to do with the young students in our elementary classrooms? Furthermore, what does this research have to do with the cultivation of critical thinking in elementary schools?

The implication for elementary educators, and educators more broadly, is that we can't just "teach critical thinking" on its own. Elementary students are actual novices in the subjects they study; the analytical and evaluative thinking processes children need should be developed in concert with growing expertise. Teachers can support students in understanding deeper concepts and structures in a discipline by providing ample opportunities for them to make meaning and draw connections in knowledge-rich environments. We need to infuse habits of thinking and talking into the content we are teaching.

We see the impact of expertise levels in the research on background knowledge in reading development. Background knowledge has a substantial impact on students' ability to comprehend what they are reading. Proficient readers experience this reality every time they venture into reading something with unfamiliar domain-specific references and jargon. They can draw upon a deep base of knowledge and are more capable of identifying the gaps in their comprehension, which makes their habits of rereading and conducting additional research more effective. Not only will individuals who lack this knowledge base struggle to understand what they are reading, but they are also far less likely to notice and revise misconceptions. Knowledge of context and vocabulary and even language structures can either support or inhibit understanding (much like in the example of *spring* earlier in the chapter). In a critical review of the studies into background knowledge's impact on reading comprehension, Smith and colleagues (2021) found readers with large vocabularies and broad background knowledge were more successful at navigating and comprehending texts, especially texts that require the reader to make a number of inferences to comprehend content. Even readers with weaker word-reading skills were more successful when they encountered texts about a familiar topic.

The importance of knowledge is especially relevant to literacy instruction, the raison d'être for elementary schools across the globe. More than 30 years ago, cognitive scientist Keith Stanovich (1986) coined the term "the

Matthew effect" to describe the role vocabulary, a proxy for knowledge, plays in the ability of readers to understand what they read. The name alludes to a parable from the Gospel of Matthew, where servants are entrusted with different amounts of their master's riches. The servant given the most was able to increase the riches, while the servant given the least was unable to add anything to what he was given. Known as the "Parable of the Talents," the story inspired the common saying first attributed to 19th century poet Percy Bysshe Shelley: "the rich get richer, the poor get poorer." The Matthew effect describes how the differences between strong and struggling readers compound over time. Children who master foundational reading skills continue to learn more and more words through rich reading experiences, while struggling readers know and learn substantially fewer words.

Nevertheless, vocabulary knowledge is not stagnant, and some early-elementary interventions could help counter the Matthew effect. In 2015, researchers from the University of Iowa and Florida State published a study that followed 485 students from kindergarten to 10th grade (Duff et al., 2015). They were specifically investigating the relationship between early word-reading skills and vocabulary knowledge later in life. The researchers found a relationship between 4th grade performance on a word-reading assessment and vocabulary knowledge in 10th grade (although the researchers noted that this relationship could also represent the result of many different types of reading activities, including independent reading outside school). The Matthew effect continues to be a "powerful framework for understanding not only vocabulary development but also response to vocabulary instruction and intervention" (Coyne et al., 2019, p. 177). But this phenomenon should not let schools off the hook. Rich and consistent vocabulary instruction (as well as discipline-specific instruction in science and social studies) should be paired with targeted interventions for students. If we can identify students who need extra support, then we can also provide them with intervention.

What About Google?

Finally, we must respond to a significant challenge posed by critics of curriculum that focuses on building knowledge rather than general critical thinking skills. In a world where so much knowledge is easily accessible through the internet, teaching factual information seems antiquated, even futile. An education advice column in *The Atlantic* recommends teachers focus on teaching learning skills rather than specific facts or details (Freireich & Platzer, 2021). More and more, the phrase "If they can google it, don't teach it" is commonly used in educational materials for teachers. Adults use the internet to learn all the time—there are countless stories of individuals teaching themselves new musical instruments and languages. If individuals are capable of learning so much on their own, shouldn't that just be part of what kids do at school?

While advances in technology are inspiring, the ability to utilize the internet for learning is not a straightforward enterprise. Even though children today may be growing up in a world with novel and engaging technologies, they are not necessarily experts at using those technologies to support their learning and understanding. Inside and outside education, media literacy is often cited as an urgent need in a world where so much conflicting information can be accessed via the internet. And it is a need, but one that exists in a wider context of literacy needs. Struggling readers will continue to face the same challenges with difficult texts, no matter what medium they read the texts in. Whether children read an article online at home or on paper in school, if they don't have the requisite background knowledge, they will struggle to comprehend the text. If we have not prepared students to approach texts on a given subject, we leave them vulnerable to accessing poor sources of information without the requisite skills to analyze them, much like the students who encountered the PISA questions on the benefits of cow's milk discussed in the Introduction.

Although there are thoughtful uses for technology, teachers should ask themselves whether using technology in the classroom will support students in deep processing of content. Technology can create access to material by offering students with specific needs audiobooks, keyboards, and alternative presentations of information. But technology used without intention can fracture students' attention necessary for deep processing. If technology distracts from or complicates the achievement of a learning goal, it is likely better to not use it at all.

Conclusion

Elementary school is an opportunity. When students are younger and content is more accessible, the differences in their background knowledge are less evident. However, as children grow, the gap in how much they have read and how much they know begins to influence how easily they can learn more. But the differences in vocabulary and background knowledge are much smaller in elementary school, especially early elementary school, than they are later in life. This means that schools can structure their instructional activities around building knowledge beginning with the early grades. The next two chapters will discuss a framework for critical thinking that teachers can use to craft ambitious visions for their classrooms.

Chapter 1 Key Points

- Critical thinking is the ability to analyze and evaluate information in order to make a judgment.

- Critical thinking is the result of content knowledge and expertise. Critical thinking cannot be distilled into a set of general, contentless skills.

- Procedural and conceptual knowledge are both important parts of building expertise. Teachers should focus on building depth of processing with both types of knowledge.

- Just because information is readily available through technological advances doesn't mean students do not need to be taught knowledge in schools.

- Elementary school is a unique opportunity to build content knowledge and expertise in core academic subjects. Even though gaps exist between students, they are significantly smaller in elementary school than they are in secondary grades.

Further Reading

I suggest the following texts for their exploration of how the brain learns to read:

- *Language at the Speed of Sight: How We Read, Why So Many Can't, and What Can Be Done About It* by Mark Seidenberg

- *Proust and the Squid: The Story and Science of the Reading Brain* by Maryanne Wolf

- *Reader, Come Home: The Reading Brain in a Digital World* by Maryanne Wolf

In addition to these books, Emily Hanford's reporting for American Public Media (https://features.apmreports.org/reading/) provides an in-depth look into the shortcomings of reading instruction as well as an approachable description of research.

For those interested in cognitive science research into memory and learning, I recommend the following:

- *Powerful Teaching: Unleash the Science of Learning* by Pooja K. Agarwal and Patrice M. Bain

- *Make It Stick: The Science of Successful Learning* by Peter C. Brown, Henry L. Roediger III, and Mark A. McDaniel

- *Made to Stick: Why Some Ideas Survive and Others Die* by Chip Heath and Dan Heath

2 INTRODUCTION TO THE CRITICAL THINKING FRAMEWORK

As discussed in Chapter 1, critical thinking is using analysis and evaluation to make a judgment. Analysis, evaluation, and judgment are not discrete skills; rather, they emerge from the accumulation of knowledge. The accumulation of knowledge does not mean students sit at desks mindlessly reciting memorized information, like in 19th century grammar schools. Our goal is not for learners to regurgitate facts by rote without demonstrating their understanding of the connections, structures, and deeper ideas embedded in the content they are learning. To foster critical thinking in school, especially for our youngest learners, we need a pedagogy that centers knowledge and also honors the ability of children to engage with knowledge.

This chapter outlines the Critical Thinking Framework: five instructional approaches educators can incorporate into their instruction to nurture deeper thinking. These approaches can also guide intellectual preparation protocols and unit unpackings to prepare rigorous, engaging instruction for elementary students. Some of these approaches, such as *reason with evidence*, will seem similar to other "contentless" programs professing to teach critical thinking skills. But others, such as *say it in your own words* or *look for structure*, are targeted at ensuring learners soundly understand content so that they can engage in complex thinking. You will likely notice that every single one of these approaches requires students to talk—to themselves, to a partner, or to the whole class. Dialogue, specifically in the context of teacher-led discussions, is essential for students to analyze, evaluate, and judge (i.e., *do critical thinking*). Later in the book, we will turn to ways to structure student talk.

The latter part of the chapter digs into what these approaches are as well as their basis in current research. Three case studies describe how the framework comes alive in classrooms. The chapter ends with a K–5 continuum showing how the framework progresses over the course of elementary school. In the next chapter, we will talk about how to plan for outcomes based on the subject.

The Critical Thinking Framework
Say It in Your Own Words

Students articulate ideas in their own words. They use unique phrasing and do not parrot the explanations of others.

When learning new material, students who pause to explain concepts in their own words (to themselves or others) demonstrate an overall better understanding than students who do not (Nokes-Malach et al., 2013). However, it's not enough for us to pause frequently and ask students to explain, especially if they are only being asked to repeat procedures. Explanations should be effortful and require students to make connections to prior knowledge and concepts as well as to revise misconceptions (Richey & Nokes-Malach, 2015).

Break It Down

Students break down the components, steps, or smaller ideas within a bigger idea or procedure.

In addition to expressing concepts in their own words, students should look at new concepts in terms of parts and wholes. For instance, when learning a new type of problem or task, students can explain the steps another student took to arrive at their answer, which promotes an understanding that transfers to other tasks with a similar underlying structure. Asking students to explain the components and rationale behind procedural steps can also lead to more flexible problem solving overall (Rittle-Johnson, 2006). By breaking down ideas into component parts, students are also better equipped to monitor the soundness of their own understanding as well as to see similar patterns (i.e., regularity) among differing tasks. For example, in writing, lessons can help students see how varying subordinating conjunction phrases at the start of sentences can support the flow and readability of a paragraph. In math, a solution can be broken down into smaller steps.

Look for Structure

Students look beyond shallow surface characteristics to see deep structures and underlying principles.

Learners struggle to see regularity in similar problems that have small differences (Reed et al., 1985). Even when students are taught how to complete one kind of task, they struggle to transfer their understanding to a new task where some of the superficial characteristics have been changed. This is because students, especially students who are novices in a domain, tend to emphasize the surface structure of a task rather than deep structure (Chi & Van Lehn, 2012).

By prompting students to notice deep structures—such as the characteristics of a genre or the needs of animals—rather than surface structures, teachers foster the development of comprehensive schemata in students' long-term memories, which they are more likely to then apply to novel situations. Teachers should monitor for student understanding of deep structures across several tasks and examples.

Notice Gaps or Inconsistencies in Ideas

Students ask questions about gaps and inconsistencies in material, arguments, and their own thinking.

When students engage in explanations of material, they are more likely to notice when they misunderstand material or to detect a conflict with their prior knowledge (Richey & Nokes-Malach, 2015). In a classroom, analyzing conflicting ideas and interpretations allows students to revise misconceptions and refine mental models. Noticing gaps and inconsistencies in information also helps students to evaluate the persuasiveness of arguments and to ask relevant questions.

Reason with Evidence

Students construct arguments with evidence and evaluate the evidence in others' reasoning.

Reasoning with evidence matters in every subject, but what counts for evidence in a mathematical proof differs from what is required in an English essay. Students should learn the rules and conventions for evidence across a wide range of disciplines in school. The habits of looking for and weighing evidence also intersect with some of the other critical thinking approaches discussed above. Noticing regularity in reasoning and structure helps learners find evidence efficiently, while attending to gaps and inconsistencies in information encourages caution before reaching hasty conclusions.

Countering Two Critiques

Some readers may be wondering how the Critical Thinking Framework differs from other general skills curricula. The framework differs in that it demands application in the context of students' content knowledge, rather than in isolation. It is a pedagogical tool to help students make sense of the content they are learning. Students should never sit through a lesson where they are told to "say things in their own words" when there is nothing to say anything about. While a contentless lesson could help on the margins, it will not be as relevant or transferable. As the case studies later in the chapter demonstrate, specific content matters. A checklist of "critical thinking skills" cannot replace deep subject knowledge. The framework should not be blindly applied to all subjects without context because results will look quite different in an ELA or science class.

Other readers may be thinking about high-stakes tests: how does the Critical Thinking Framework fit in with an overwhelming emphasis on assessments aligned to national or state standards? This is a valid concern and an important point to address. For teachers, schools, and districts locked into an accountability system that values performance on state tests but does not communicate content expectations beyond general standards, the arguments I make may seem beside the point. Sure, knowledge matters, but the curriculum demands that students know how to quickly identify the main idea of a paragraph, even if they don't have any background knowledge about the topic of the paragraph.

It is crucial that elementary practitioners be connected to both evolving research on learning and the limiting realities we teach within. Unfortunately, I can provide no easy answers beyond saying that teaching is a balancing act. The tension, while real and relevant to teachers' daily lives, should not cloud our vision for what children need from their school experiences.

I also argue it is easier to incorporate the demands of our current standardized testing environment into a curriculum rich with history, science, art, geography, languages, and novels than the reverse. In the next chapter, we will discuss building an ambitious vision for student learning and defining critical thinking outcomes. The Critical Thinking Framework presents ways to approach all kinds of knowledge in a way that presses students toward deeper processing of the content they are learning. If we can raise the bar for student work and thinking in our classrooms, the question of how students perform on standardized tests will become secondary to helping them achieve much loftier and important goals. The choice of whether to emphasize excellent curriculum or high-stakes tests, insofar as it is a choice at all, should never be existential or a zero-sum game.

The three case studies that follow will help you put yourself in the minds of your students and plan for the kind of thinking we want to see. Whether you are an early-, middle-, or upper-elementary teacher, or you specialize in math, ELA, or science, you should see an example that is relevant to your daily experiences.

Case Studies

As we've already discussed, critical thinking is not a general set of skills easily separated from discipline-specific knowledge. To represent the Critical Thinking Framework's approach in action, I provide three case studies that illustrate how teachers can use the framework to support deep processing and content mastery.

The case studies illustrate how elementary students may articulate their understanding. I like to call this planning for "kid speech." It is crucial for educators to have a clear vision of what we want students to say and do in our lessons and, most important, to bear in mind that children will rarely express themselves with the exact same words as adults. In fact, we *do not want* children to repeat ideas in the same manner as adults. Children need to take on the cognitive work of articulating their ideas in words and phrases that make sense to them. When preparing for how students will express the ideas of a lesson or unit in their own words, we need to parse the difference between how adults explain the concepts and how the young students in our classrooms will explain the concepts. See Figure 2.1 for a comparison of adult speech and student speech related to partitioning a unit into fractions.

FIGURE 2.1

Comparison of Adult and Student Descriptions of 1st Grade Math Content

Adult Speech	Student Speech
In this unit, students are working on understanding how to accurately partition shapes to create halves and fourths.	The pieces are the same size.
Halves are made when a shape is partitioned into two equal parts.	Halves are when there are two pieces of the same size.
Fourths are made when a shape is partitioned into four equal parts.	Fourths are when there are four pieces that are the same size.
Fourths can also be called quarters.	Fourths are also called quarters. That's probably like how you also need four quarters to make a dollar.
Students will need to see that halves and fourths are the same shapes and size.	I have to make lines through the center so the parts are the same size. When I don't draw through the center, they are different sizes and shapes.
The more a shape is partitioned, the smaller the parts become. There is an inverse relationship between the number of parts and the size of the parts.	When I have more pieces, the pieces are smaller. When I have fewer pieces, the pieces are bigger.

Newer teachers may have more difficulty imagining exactly how a 1st grader or a 4th grader may explain their thinking in their own, unique phrasing. Even experienced teachers may struggle with this process if they have switched grades or retooled their expectations. Although the purpose of this exercise is to be prepared for what students may say, it is unlikely we can anticipate every exact word. That's OK! We don't want to miss the proverbial forest for the trees. Once you know what understanding can sound like, it is easier to identify the great thinking embedded in a student's explanation or in their response to a question.

The case studies predict what students might say and provide examples for how the Critical Thinking Framework can come to life in the classroom. It's not enough to point to research about this or that strategy; we need to get concrete about what the framework sounds like in practice. As you read the case studies, think about how students in your class or school might articulate their understanding.

Mr. Donovan's 2nd Grade ELA Class

Mr. Donovan's 2nd graders are learning about the landforms and geography of New York City. By the end of the unit, they will research one borough or river in depth and write an informational paragraph presenting their learning.

At the beginning of the unit, Mr. Donovan builds student knowledge by teaching the definitions of *borough, river, island, coast,* and *ocean*. He also teaches his students about cardinal directions and how compass points work on a map. They create maps of their classroom and the hallway to practice simple map creation.

Mr. Donovan engages the students in regular review of these definitions because they are critical to the work students will do later in the unit. During turn-and-talks and writing activities, he asks students to explain the definitions *in their own words*. Students explain the vocabulary by saying the following:

- "A borough is like smaller towns inside a city."
- "A borough is a big section of a city."
- "A river is a stream of water that connects to the sea, a lake, or another stream of water."
- "An island is land surrounded by water on all sides."
- "The coast is the edge of the land by the water."

- "The coast is the part of the land that is by the sea."

- "An ocean is a large body of water."

- "There are five big bodies of saltwater that cover the Earth."

At different stopping points, Mr. Donovan wants to make sure his students not only know the information but can *recognize the deep structures* underlying the vocabulary definitions and apply them in a new context. Once the instruction turns from types of landforms to the features of New York City in particular, students apply the definitions within the context of the city. They say things like the following:

- "New York City's coast is on the Atlantic Ocean."

- "The Bronx is the only borough that isn't on an island."

- "The Harlem River connects to the Hudson River and the East River."

- "Staten Island is south of all the other boroughs. It's connected by a bridge to Brooklyn, which is part of a larger island."

Given a blank map of New York City, students can identify the location of boroughs, rivers, islands, and oceans. They can use cardinal directions to describe the map. They show evidence of their learning by making the following statements:

- "The Bronx is the most north."

- "Brooklyn is south of Queens."

- "The Hudson River is on the west side of Manhattan."

- "Manhattan is on the west side of the East River. Brooklyn is on the east side of the East River."

As student knowledge deepens, Mr. Donovan asks questions that require students to retrieve and *apply relevant facts as evidence* for their conclusions. Students respond to questions like "Why does New York City have more than 2,000 bridges and tunnels?" One says, "All of New York City's boroughs are part of islands, except the Bronx. The city needs bridges and tunnels to go over and under the Hudson River, the East River, and the Harlem River. This helps keep all parts of the city connected."

As the students learn more about the boroughs, they share what they learned by writing informational paragraphs with a topic sentence, two supporting details, and a conclusion sentence. They create outlines that *break down the components* of a paragraph.

Since writing a strong paragraph is an important 2nd grade goal as well as a critical foundation for future writing, Mr. Donovan ensures students have enough time to look at exemplar paragraphs and practice revising paragraphs with errors. Once students understand the components of a quality paragraph, he presents the class with incomplete paragraphs or paragraphs containing common mistakes. He wants students to *notice the gaps and inconsistencies* in the practice examples before they revise their own paragraphs. He also presents a paragraph with lots of details about Staten Island, but the information is not organized into a structured paragraph. During a turn-and-talk, a few students share their observations, such as "This paragraph is sharing a lot of facts about Staten Island, but it doesn't have a topic sentence saying what the paragraph is about." The class works together to improve the paragraph.

Ms. Halpert's 1st Grade Math Class

In Ms. Halpert's 1st grade class, students are studying fractions by partitioning circles and rectangles into halves and fourths. Although she wants them to understand the procedure of partitioning shapes, she also wants students to grasp that the more they partition a shape, the smaller the shares become. She knows this concept will help students access more difficult fraction standards later.

Once students understand that fractional parts are equal, she helps students *break down* the partitioning process for shapes. When they discuss examples and nonexamples of fractional partitions, she asks students to explain the steps and the rationale behind the steps. One student responds, "I have to make sure my parts are the same size and shape so they will be equal. If I make one of the fourths a different size, then all the parts won't be equal."

Ms. Halpert also asks students to critique incorrect work so they can *notice gaps and inconsistencies* in their own work. She presents students with two pieces of student work: in one, where the student drew lines through the center to create halves; in the other, the student did not. She asks the class which work sample they agree with and why. She challenges them to explain what feedback they would give to the incorrect student. They respond, "The second student's work didn't actually make two equal parts. They made a line *to* the side of the center, not *through* the center."

After students practice partitioning the same shapes into halves and fourths, Ms. Halpert asks students to look at two rectangles, one partitioned into halves and the other partitioned into fourths. She asks students to consider the following problem: "Damon and Rory decide to share a brownie by cutting it in half. At another table, Henry, Zach, Penny, and Bella also share a brownie by cutting it in quarters. Damon is upset because he thinks that the other table had more brownie because they had more pieces. Is Damon right?"

Most students say Damon is wrong, but Ms. Halpert asks students to *explain their reasoning with evidence.* The students say the following:

- "Damon is wrong. When you cut something into more pieces, the pieces get smaller."
- "The other table actually had less brownie. Damon and Rory only had to cut their brownie in half, so their pieces are actually bigger than the other table."

Ms. Halpert then asks students to go further and think about a pattern or rule that would always apply to situations like Damon's. The teacher wants students to understand the *underlying structure and principles* of fractional parts. Students come up with a couple ways of expressing the rule:

- "When I have more pieces, the pieces are smaller. When I have fewer pieces, the pieces are bigger."
- "After I make halves, I can halve them again. This makes fourths. Fourths are like half of half."

Ms. Katz's 4th Grade Science Class

Ms. Katz's 4th graders are building their foundational understanding of electricity. In this unit, they are learning about the properties of materials that act as insulators and conductors. They can describe the purpose of insulators and conductors in an electric circuit.

Ms. Katz teaches her students the essential vocabulary they need to know through explicit instruction, read-alouds, and hands-on demonstrations. To ensure her students understand the characteristics of insulators and conductors, she regularly asks them to write or verbally *explain the definitions in their own words.* She hears students say:

- "A conductor is a material that completes an electric circuit."
- "A conductor lets electricity flow through it."
- "An insulator slows down or stops an electric current. It doesn't let the electricity flow."
- "Insulators don't complete a circuit, so the energy doesn't flow."
- "You have to have a conductor in a circuit to let the energy flow, but the insulator protects people by not allowing the electricity to flow everywhere."

Through instruction and experimentation, students are able to categorize materials based on whether they conduct or insulate electricity. They *notice the repetitive characteristics* that make a material an insulator or a conductor:

- "Metals are conductors, like aluminum, copper, and steel. I can use these in a circuit to keep the electricity flowing."
- "Plastics, rubber, glass, and dry wood are insulators. I can use these to stop or slow the flow of electricity."

During labs, students learn how to build circuits. They can *break down the components* of a circuit:

- "I know I need an energy source where the electricity comes from. This could be a battery. I also need a way to get the energy flowing, so I need a material that is a conductor. That's why I can use copper wire because it's a metal and metals conduct electricity."
- "I don't want electricity to flow outside this circuit, so I have to make sure I have insulators so the electricity can't make another circuit. This could be really dangerous!"

Ms. Katz understands that there are a number of misconceptions or confusing scenarios with the potential to stump students. Rather than shy away from the challenge, she makes sure to proactively pose questions to students so they can address difficult topics as a class:

- "Why is only dry wood an insulator? How wet does wood need to be to conduct electricity? Let's look into that."

- "I notice when I use this steel nail I can complete a circuit, but it doesn't work when I use the piece of rubber. Why is there a difference?"

Students write lab reports after investigating whether materials are conductors or insulators. They support their thinking with specific findings (*reasoning with evidence*). One student writes:

- "Metals are conductors. When I tested aluminum, copper, and steel, all of them helped complete the circuit, so the electricity flowed through them."

Critical Thinking in Elementary School

You may read the case studies and immediately react with "Oh, I can do that!" Others may disagree. Some teachers may believe that elementary students are too young to engage in this kind of work. To them, building domain knowledge and implementing the Critical Thinking Framework seem beyond the scope of those grades, if not downright developmentally inappropriate. For so many educators, our schools and teaching programs have emphasized the necessity of "developmentally appropriate" instruction. Unfortunately, that term is not as useful as it once seemed.

We can trace the origin of the term *developmental appropriateness* to groundbreaking psychologist Jean Piaget, who proposed four distinct stages of child development. He hypothesized that when students are in a specific cognitive stage, they cannot engage in the intellectual tasks of a more advanced stage. While there is a developmental continuum of learning and development, there is a high degree of variability among children, and clear breaks between stages of development are not necessarily distinguishable (Siegler, 1994). Moreover, just because a topic or way of thinking may be unfamiliar to a child doesn't mean the topic or thinking is in itself inappropriate. Perhaps "the students are missing the necessary background knowledge. Or maybe a different presentation of the same material would make it easier to understand" (Willingham, 2008, p. 39).

As educators, we can carefully plan knowledge and skills instruction (see Chapter 3) and use the Critical Thinking Framework to help students deeply process the content they are learning. Our mission is not to overwhelm children with complexity, but to use our lessons to create an environment where they can engage in rigorous and productive thinking. Instead of asking whether a lesson is appropriate, educators should ask whether their lesson builds access to, and provides opportunities for making meaning of, complex topics. Students may require a series of lessons, rather than just a single lesson, to build the foundational understanding required to engage in a complex task. We will explore ways to structure our lessons to do just that in Chapter 4.

Critical Thinking Framework, K–5 ELA and Math Trajectory

Let's look at an example of an ELA and math trajectory for the Critical Thinking Framework that outlines how each critical thinking approach can support students in early, middle, and late elementary school. This trajectory is not prescriptive for how every school should enact the framework; instead, think of it as a model for thinking about and planning for K–5 alignment. While the case studies provided a snapshot of student thinking in specific units, the trajectory offers a bird's-eye view for how critical thinking expectations should grow over the course of several grades. When older students struggle with these critical thinking approaches, the descriptions of the progression through younger grades can suggest ways to scaffold the thinking processes to assist them.

The framework does not stand on its own without subject-specific content. While I use general language to describe its evolution, especially in ELA, you should remember that students should be learning real stuff, like science and social studies. The approaches will help you increase the depth of processing while students learn content.

Say It in Your Own Words

Students articulate ideas in their own words. They use unique phrasing and do not parrot the explanations of others.

ELA

For our youngest students, learning to summarize stories, texts, and ideas is crucial. Often, young students will repeat the same exact words from a story or used by an adult. They will need models, examples, and prompts to help them use their own words to summarize and retell. Through drawing, graphic organizers, and discussion, 5- and 6-year-olds can offer their own explanations and descriptions of different ideas.

In the middle grades, students still need to summarize and retell ideas in their own words, but their summaries should be infused with more inferential thinking. They may notice similarities and differences among texts and characters as well as describe different perspectives or points of view. Students in the middle grades should also be listening closely to one another so they can summarize one another's points. Not only does this practice demonstrate active listening and understanding, it is also the foundation for children determining whether they agree with an idea, disagree, or need further clarification.

In the upper grades, students contextualize words and phrases to describe characters, an author's point of view, or the craft evident in a particular passage. They are able to notice and explain an author's choice of words. Their summaries include larger themes and messages in a text. At this age, they can integrate information from multiple text sources to share research findings or to pose new questions. They are able to distinguish between key information and ancillary points. In discussions with their peers, 4th and 5th graders should be continuing to listen closely to their peers so they can summarize their points as well as synthesize multiple contributions to the conversation.

Math

When kindergartners start interacting with counting sets, they can express how they counted and what those numbers mean. For instance, they may say, "When I touch a new cube, I count another one." They can answer questions about the numbers they are counting and what they know about those numbers. They can explain while counting how they know the total number they counted based on the number they added on. Similar explanations can be given when doing basic addition and subtraction, where students can explain when they are joining numbers together or separating numbers to result in a smaller final number. The same sorts of explanations extend to descriptions of shapes, where they see them in their environments, and the characteristics that help them identify the shapes. First graders build on these explanations with larger numbers within 120. They start counting not just by 1s but by 10s, 5s, and 2s. They explain their understanding of number values in plain terms, like groups of 10.

By 2nd and 3rd grade, students' explanations expand to include richer explanations about problems they are solving, which they can express and describe in their own words. They can use their prior knowledge of counting to describe characteristics of even and odd numbers. They rely on pictorial and increasingly abstract models to show their thinking and demonstrate individual understanding of the taught concepts. In these grades, students employ discipline-specific vocabulary like *sum, product,* and *quotient* with explanations that demonstrate they understand the appropriate contexts to use the words.

In the upper grades, students are using more and more discipline vocabulary to describe problems and approaches to problem solving. They use appropriate tools and representations to construct their explanations.

Break It Down

Students break down the components, steps, or smaller ideas within a bigger idea or procedure.

ELA

In kindergarten and 1st grade, children are introduced to genres like fiction and nonfiction, storytelling structures like problem and solution, and the different roles of authors or illustrators. In discussions about the texts they read, even the youngest students can look at a text and break down the characteristics of a genre. They can provide justifications based on what they have learned. In these grades, students can respond to questions about characters' feelings and motivations, which will require them to think about what the characters said or did in the story. They will be able to describe the connections with text structures, such as how the solution resolves the problem in a story or how a character is able to achieve a goal. Even in informational texts, students can explain how an author introduces a topic and provides facts as well as the role text features play in filling in gaps in information.

Students continue to expand their understanding of different genres and text structures in the middle elementary grades. They can notice the smaller choices authors make to incorporate characteristics of a genre. In response to questions about fictional texts, they explain central messages and where they are communicated in the text. They can break down the topic of a nonfiction text by pointing out the smaller components and steps. In discussions with their teacher and peers, students describe the connections between several events in a story or informational text. When tracking the development of a character, they look for smaller details and moments throughout a given text. They can describe the steps of making inferences by pointing to specific points in a text.

Students in the upper grades are reading and discussing longer texts of greater complexity. They can break down how word choice and syntax communicate an author's tone or mood. When describing fiction and informational texts, they can look at the whole as a compilation of many parts and describe the purposes of the different parts. They look at point of view, arguments, and character development as creations of the author using constituent parts. They are comfortable parsing texts for these smaller components. When explaining their thinking to others, older students carefully track how they reached their conclusions. They can share these thinking steps and evaluate the thinking steps of others.

Math

Kindergarten and 1st grade students can break down the components of tactile and pictorial representations. They can fluently explain how numbers can be deconstructed into smaller numbers and represent the components of numbers through number bonds, bar models, and equations. This same thinking applies to fractional representations, telling time, and modeling shapes with smaller shapes.

In the middle grades, students become more fluent in decomposing and recomposing numbers according to their place values. This fluency supports the ability to group and regroup 10s, especially when students are adding and subtracting two- and three-digit numbers. Similarly, students notice multiplicative relationships among repeated groups of numbers, which can be represented with arrays. These relationships can be broken down into groups, a number of columns and rows, or with a number sentence. Students can break down and rewrite division and multiplication problems based on the relationships between multiplication and division.

In the upper grades, students can effortlessly move between verbal and abstract representations of multiplication and division. They see the relationships between large numbers by using place value components, like $700/70 = 10$. They can similarly decompose and recompose fractional representations. They can describe $3/16$ as the same as $1/16$ three times, and they use these types of relationships to solve increasingly complex problems.

Look for Structure

Students look beyond shallow surface characteristics to see deep structures and underlying principles.

ELA

Kindergartners and 1st graders are introduced to the structures of storybooks, poetry, and informational texts. Teachers point out and discuss with students consistent characteristics, like story elements and nonfiction text features, which they use to deepen their understanding and locate important information. As students read books within and across genres, they engage in discussions comparing and contrasting similar texts. They learn to write a complete sentence with a subject and a predicate. As they master sentence writing, they also begin to write more than one sentence in their own narrative, persuasive, and informational pieces. They read books across genres so they can replicate the structures they encounter in books in their own writing.

Second and 3rd graders expand upon their earlier foundation by noticing repetitive structures and characteristics in texts and start to recognize and explain how subgenres, like mysteries and biographies, also have their own unique arrangements. These students further use their understanding of text structures to describe relationships between parts of a text, such as cause and effect, steps in a sequence, and problem and solution. When they encounter new texts, they are able to use these mental models to deepen their understanding of the content. In their writing, students develop an appreciation for the craft behind the writing. Students notice and understand the ways authors make specific choices when they include dialogue and descriptive language, and they replicate these craft moves in their own writing.

Fourth and 5th graders use their extensive understanding of different genre forms to compare and contrast the treatment of similar themes and topics. They can find patterns within a text that represent characteristics of that genre, which they use to make inferences about the author's intentions. Older students closely read texts to identify the specific craft moves of the author. They can describe the purpose and impact of rhythm and alliteration in poems and look for figurative language, stage directions, dialogue, settings, and character descriptions in drama and prose texts. Students notice when an author creates a point of view or shifts point of view in the text. They can describe the purpose and impact of these authorial choices. Fourth and 5th graders also engage with longer, complex texts where they need to describe how the parts (e.g., chapters, sections, steps, procedures, directions, stanzas, acts) fit together to create a whole.

Math

Kindergartners and 1st graders use the structural regularities of the base-10 number system to build fluency with counting. They start to notice that there are multiple ways of putting together different numbers, such as 10, and that these combinations regularly repeat for decade numbers up to 120 (e.g., 3 + 7 = 10 and 23 + 7 = 30). Similarly, shapes such as hexagons and trapezoids can be decomposed into smaller shapes (e.g., triangles). The repetitive relationships are described and discussed.

Students in the middle elementary grades build on skills learned in earlier grades by applying number patterns to the 1,000s. They not only notice arithmetic patterns when adding and subtracting but also notice multiplicative patterns. For instance, when numbers are multiplied by even numbers, the resulting numbers will always be even. In terms of shapes, categories become more subtle, and students are attentive to a wider range of characteristics to distinguish between quadrilaterals and rectangles. Students also notice structural regularities across topics. Measuring area and perimeter are related to multiplication and addition.

In 4th and 5th grade, students independently generate patterns according to different rules, including patterns with alternating rules. Students are able to explain how the pattern is regular. They also bring together discrete skills to represent patterns, such as creating line graphs to represent fractional relationships or data sets. They apply their understanding of addition and subtraction to describe shapes according to their angle measure. They even describe the relationships between fraction and decimal representations. They see the patterns in how a decimal is the same value as a fraction.

Notice Gaps or Inconsistencies in Ideas

Students ask questions about gaps and inconsistencies in material, arguments, and their own thinking.

ELA

In the earliest grades, teachers model pausing in a book or a discussion to ask a question or point out an area of confusion. Students begin to formulate their own questions based on what they already know, what they want to learn more about, and what still might not make sense for them. This is also part of the prediction process, where students think about what they already know and what they think might be the case later in a text.

In the middle grades, teachers begin to transfer more questioning responsibility to students. Students have more opportunities to formulate questions without teacher support. Moreover, teachers model how to engage in discussions where participants listen closely to one another. When something doesn't quite make sense or has a missing piece, students learn to pause and ask questions. Students are also given more opportunities in their writing to construct and critique opinions. They reflect on ways to strengthen and revise their arguments. They are also encouraged to critique the reasoning of the authors they read.

By 4th and 5th grade, students frequently refine their thinking through discussion. Teachers prompt students to look at their own and their peers' ideas for more subtle conclusions or alternative explanations. Writing projects build in reflective processes, like peer feedback and revision. In these grades, students are often asked to question and critique the arguments and ideas presented by authors.

Math

While students are counting sets, they notice irregularities and errors that do not correspond with base-10 patterns. Even the youngest students notice the regular repetition of 0–9, and they can describe when that pattern is not honored in an example. In addition to using their counting fluency to critique and revise errors, the youngest mathematicians can look at simple addition and subtraction problems to determine whether or not they are true. In describing the meaning of the equal sign, students can notice when an inaccurate number sentence is written. Similar to counting errors, untrue number sentences can be revised to become true.

Second and 3rd graders continue this critical stance by evaluating their work and the work of others. They can describe the steps taken to solve a problem as well as steps that may have gone awry. In these grades, students engage with more data representations such as bar graphs and pictographs. Students can determine the validity of inferences made based on the data set. They can also discuss what information may be missing, or the kinds of surveys they would need to conduct to answer posed questions.

Finally, in the upper grades, students are able to critically examine their work and the work of others to determine areas that may need revision or improvement. They can pose questions about where in a problem they are stuck, or the parts of an explanation that make sense. Most problems by 5th grade are multistep problems, so students can break problems down according to when they know their next steps and when they do not.

Reason with Evidence

Students construct arguments with evidence and evaluate the evidence in others' reasoning.

ELA

In kindergarten, students are asked to explain where they get their ideas by paraphrasing a part of the story or picking a detail out of a picture. Kids are always prompted to fully explain their thinking using words such as *so* and *because*. By 1st grade, students are comfortable pointing out places in a text that support their ideas.

In 2nd and 3rd grade, students transition from supporting their ideas by paraphrasing to picking out specific sentences and phrases from a text. They can discriminate between strong and weak evidence examples. They can look at a piece of writing and determine ways to improve the quality of its evidence. They notice when the writer uses irrelevant details.

By the end of elementary school, students are comfortable selecting precise evidence. They are even able to point out what elements in their sentence-level evidence best support their ideas. Class discussions evaluate what makes evidence stronger and more persuasive. Students also are comfortable with the idea that there can be more than one perspective or "correct" answer. The evidence they select or choose to emphasize may lead to different conclusions, especially when deliberating about a complex text.

Math

In the earliest grades, students can verbally justify their strategies for counting and solving problems by describing steps taken with pictures or concrete tools. They can verbalize mental strategies for solving addition and subtraction problems.

Starting in the middle grades, students can describe their strategies and reasoning in writing, though these explanations may be supported with sentence frames. They apply similar skills from ELA to their math explanations. They reflect on the strength of their reasoning, and they can discriminate between strong and weak evidence. For instance, they may be presented with a scenario where they need to determine a correct solution to a problem. In their explanation, they explain not only which answer is correct but also why the other solution doesn't work.

By the end of elementary school, students employ an array of tools to present their reasoning, orally and in writing. They flexibly use examples and nonexamples to illustrate why a strategy or tool was appropriate for a problem. They can analyze others' work, pinpointing what worked and what didn't work. They have internalized that their explanations must always include a "why," and they can cite concrete details to support their conclusions.

Conclusion

The Critical Thinking Framework is a tool teachers can use to foster analysis, evaluation, and judgment in their lessons. However, it cannot be overstated that students need to learn sufficient content to analyze, evaluate, and judge. A curriculum where students do not receive consistent instruction in knowledge-based subjects such as history or science will not yield deeper thinking. Imagine that the information contained in the curriculum is flour and the framework a fine-mesh sieve. Flour worked through the sieve comes out airier, contributing to a higher quality baked good. The framework helps teachers and students engage in deep processing for meaningful, transferable, high-quality learning.

Chapter 2 Key Points

- The Critical Thinking Framework is not a list of general skills but a tool to be embedded in content-rich lessons to encourage deeper processing.
- When planning to use the framework, predict how students will articulate their ideas. Plan for "student speech," not the way adults talk.
- The term *developmentally appropriate* is often used to judge, incorrectly, that students are not capable of academic work. Students can learn about many topics when taught background knowledge in clear, accessible chunks.
- We can scaffold the Critical Thinking Framework across a K–5 trajectory to build greater fluency and deeper understanding.

3 CREATING AN AMBITIOUS VISION FOR STUDENT OUTCOMES

Let's look at two examples of a kindergarten lesson on weather.

Example 1

Students were given the task to go outside and look at the clouds. They noticed that some clouds are big and fluffy, while other clouds are thin and wispy. Inside, they have a chart where they keep track of sunny, cloudy, and rainy days. The students create drawings and dioramas of the sky on different days. They display their artwork in the hallway. The lesson plans cite a Next Generation Science Standard for kindergarten: "Use and share observations of local weather conditions to describe patterns over time."

Example 2

Kindergarten students go outside to make observations of the sky. They draw the different types of clouds they see. The teacher asks questions such as "How are these clouds similar and different?" The teacher posts the drawings on the wall while the students read a short text about clouds. The kids learn specific names for clouds like *stratus, cirrus,* and *cumulus.* They look at their drawings and start identifying types of clouds in their drawings. The class tracks the weather each day, and students start noticing that on dark, gloomy days, they usually see stratus clouds. The teacher shares the weather forecast for the next day, and students predict the kinds of clouds they might see.

The activities described in each lesson are not so different. On the surface, they are almost identical. Students observe and draw different sorts of clouds; they track the weather. Yet the second teacher asks students to analyze the similarities and differences among the clouds. The students learn academic vocabulary to describe their observations, which grows their internal schemata for weather and clouds. They then evaluate the weather based on what they know and make predictions. With a few changes, the first classroom could easily become the second. Those few changes have students thinking more deeply and critically about what they are learning. Both teachers have a vision for the kind of work and thinking students will do, but the teacher in the second example leads students on a much more ambitious path. As students build their knowledge and expertise, they also *analyze, evaluate,* and *judge.*

Students need something to think critically about. In a meta-analysis of critical thinking studies, critical thinking instruction embedded in content instruction yielded stronger knowledge and critical thinking gains (Abrami et al., 2015). As discussed in Chapter 1, those with more specific content knowledge in a field are more capable of thinking critically than novices with little or no relevant content knowledge. However, critical thinking does not simply transfer from one context to another. It is the by-product of building schemata within a field of study. In other words, we cannot expect students to think critically without also ensuring they have learned a lot about a given topic.

Inevitably, teachers are constrained by the ages of the pupils they teach. No matter the grade, students enter the classroom with a variety of experiences with instruction and different levels of prior knowledge. As teachers, we need to strike a balance of providing students with the rigorous grade-level instruction they deserve while simultaneously adding the precise support they need to thrive. It is extremely difficult to do the latter without knowing the former. We as teachers and school leaders need to first define the outcomes our instruction is driving toward, and that means planning for the specific content and skills we want students to learn. Because critical thinking depends on the development of knowledge, schools need a systematic approach in their curriculum for setting ambitious goals and building knowledge.

For this reason, before a school or teacher can implement the Critical Thinking Framework, they need to address the academic learning goals of the curriculum. By establishing ambitious learning goals along with a curriculum that emphasizes knowledge, schools can nurture the development of critical thinking in the subjects students are learning about.

Invest in High-Quality Curriculum

Throughout this chapter, I will address one of the limiting realities of teaching: the access to and quality of curriculum. Sometimes teachers are given high-quality materials that need little revision to align to the needs of students. Sometimes, like in my first years of teaching, *none* are provided. More often, teachers are working with materials of varying depth and relevance. Before I address those needs—which are serious ones—it is crucial that I speak to the primary need for a strong curriculum. Even in a school where teachers enjoy wide-ranging autonomy over how to implement the curriculum, teachers are better off with established parameters and rich source material. It is always better to work with abundant resources than none at all.

Curriculum selection must be done at a school and district level. Individual teachers cannot be responsible for choosing a curriculum in addition to all of their other duties. Executing effective lessons, responding to student learning and misunderstanding, cultivating a positive classroom climate, maintaining healthy relationships and communication with families— these are but a few of a teacher's responsibilities. Building a curriculum from scratch should not be added to the list.

When selecting a curriculum, elementary school leaders should consider the following questions:

- Is there a scope and sequence that systematically builds knowledge in the subject area over the course of several years? Will students leave the early grades prepared to learn and master the material taught in 4th and 5th grade?

- Are the materials aligned to the best available evidence for how that subject should be taught?

- Are the teacher information guides accessible for practitioners? How easily and sustainably can teachers read and execute the curriculum?

There are a number of other considerations. Does the curriculum reflect the diversity of the community? Does the school schedule provide ample time to implement the lessons? Have other schools tried the curriculum? What were their results? All of these questions matter, but they are easier to answer once the primary three are addressed. Because curricula are designed to work in general settings, schools are unlikely to find something that accounts for every one of their unique needs. Schools and teachers can discuss adapting the chosen curriculum to make it a better fit for their specific context.

Schools and districts can take advantage of external resources to help them assess the quality of a curriculum. EdReports (https://edreports.org) provides reviews on standards alignment and teacher usability. The organization Knowledge Matters (https://knowledgematters.com) also makes recommendations regarding high-quality curricula. What Works Clearinghouse (WWC), created by the Institute of Education Sciences within the U.S. Department of Education, puts out regular reports synthesizing best practices evidenced by research. For elementary schools, WWC has shared several practice guides outlining recommendations for reading, math, writing, English language learners, Response to Intervention, and even classroom management. These resources are free and available online (https://ies .ed.gov/ncee/wwc).

Expand Our Definition of Possible

In the Introduction, I advocated for all educators to expand our definition of possible. In the example weather lessons, the second kindergarten teacher expanded the definition of possible by asking students to learn more content and engage in deeper processing of the content. But none of those actions happened spontaneously. From planning vocabulary instruction to constructing questions to sequencing the learning tasks, quite a bit of preparation went into the second kindergarten weather unit.

Although some schools and districts spend copious amounts on curriculum materials to alleviate the planning burden on teachers, many teachers are left on their own to do much of this preparation. More high-quality curriculum options are available for schools than ever before, but that doesn't mean schools purchase them. Even when schools do purchase quality curricula, they may not have systems in place to support implementation. Some teachers may be directed to read scripted lesson plans containing rigorous tasks and questioning and not have a clue of how to go about executing the lessons.

Throughout this chapter, we will check in on the experiences of two different teachers. Mr. Matthews and Ms. Pierre are each facing a scenario that teachers may encounter. One is working with a curriculum that is of high quality but needs to be tweaked to fit students' needs. The other is dealing with resources of uneven quality, filling in gaps to the best of her ability.

Mr. Matthews is a 2nd grade teacher. His school adopted an open-source, knowledge-rich curriculum for ELA. While teaching the curriculum, Mr. Matthews notices some units are stronger than others. In some places, the expectations for student work are too low for the 2nd grade, especially for writing. He knows in upper-elementary and middle school, his students will be asked to write extended pieces independently, and he wants to ensure they are prepared to do that work.

Ms. Pierre is a 3rd grade teacher. While her school has sent her to trainings on math instruction, the school does not use any single curriculum. When she joined the school, she was given access to a folder that contained lesson plans from past years, some of which came from a professionally developed curriculum and others that teachers created with resources from the internet. When she reached out to her school leadership team for guidance on determining what to teach, she was directed to the state standards. She knows 3rd grade math is a critical checkpoint for future math standards, and she wants to ensure her students are leaving 3rd grade with a firm foundation.

Despite their differing contexts, both teachers have an ambitious vision for their students. Mr. Matthews and Ms. Pierre are stand-ins for experiences very close to my own at different points in my career, and I suspect their situations mirror those of many teachers. I will share how these teachers create their ambitious vision and apply it within their own classrooms.

Create an Ambitious Vision

For the rest of the chapter, I will outline a process that teachers, grade-level teams, and leaders focused on curriculum can use to craft and execute an ambitious vision for student outcomes at their school:

- Analyze exemplar student work for ambitious goal setting.

- Define the specific domain knowledge students will learn.

- Determine what prerequisite knowledge students will need and make a plan for students who are missing prerequisites.

This process will allow teachers to expand their definition of possible by raising expectations for student performance and providing teachers with a clear picture of what students need to learn.

Before we proceed, I want to note that the sequence of steps is based on what has worked best in my own teaching practice. Some teachers may prefer to look at student work exemplars later in the process, or they may choose to emphasize certain subcomponents of the process more than others. As I shared in the opening of the book, these integrated processes can often happen simultaneously. For some teachers, certain components will stand out more than others. As always, I encourage readers to think critically about how the entire process or individual elements can help them elevate and refine their own practices.

Use Student Work Exemplars for Ambitious Goal Setting

One of the defining characteristics of any elementary curriculum is the concept of grade levels. Materials delineate what is appropriate for kindergarten versus 1st grade, and so on. Most high-level curriculum planning hinges on this fundamental understanding of what a child's performance looks like at a particular age.

As a teacher, I started in 2nd grade; over the years, I made my way to 1st grade and, eventually, kindergarten. Working with younger and younger children, I came to understand that although every student needed a foundation of reading, writing, and counting from the beginning of kindergarten, there was no "grade-level" ceiling to limit a child's growth. The only limits were the ones I imposed. As a result, even as the age of my students decreased, my expectations skyrocketed. When I took on teaching 3rd grade after years of working with 5- to 7-year-olds, I realized even more acutely that I needed to expand my definition of possible for all my students.

When we create an ambitious vision for instruction, we have to remain open to audacious goals. Before we look at a unit or anything else, we first need to think about the kind of work students *can* produce. We need to move beyond our assumptions of what students will produce or what they have produced in our classrooms previously. We start with what is possible in the broadest sense.

In addition to looking at what a high-quality exemplar looks like for a specific grade and discipline by the end of the year, it is important to look at what high-quality student work looks like for the grades above and below the one being taught. This is useful for a couple of reasons. Looking at a range of student work helps teachers avoid creating exemplars that represent too low a bar for their grade. If a teacher notices that their exemplar looks a lot like one from the grade below, then they need to revise and heighten their expectations. Also, when teachers see student work as a spectrum rather than a static line, they can make informed decisions about how to prepare students for future learning as well as the appropriate way to scaffold tasks when students struggle. Teachers should scaffold tasks to help students reach the more ambitious outcome.

Usually, teachers will turn to student work being produced within their school community for information. Schools without organized curricula or a vision for student work, however, can benefit from analyzing the work produced by other schools. Online resources can help you find a range of student work examples. For upper-elementary students, the Massachusetts Department of Education and New York State Education Department release rubric-scored student work for their annual high-stakes tests (www.doe .mass.edu/mcas/release.html; www.nysed.gov/state-assessment/past-grades-3-8-tests). The Achieve the Core website features K–12 student writing spanning narrative, informational, and persuasive genres (https://achievethecore .org/category/330/student-writing-samples). When building your ambitious vision, select three to four samples to analyze. Stay focused on what is *possible,* not what roadblocks prevent your students from meeting similar expectations. There is plenty of time to think about the roadblocks later, but you cannot figure out directions and navigation until you first pick a destination.

Analyze the Exemplar Work

Now that you have a selection of student work, make a checklist of characteristics. Avoid ambiguous observations like "neat" or "big vocabulary." Approach the student work like a delicate excavation at an archeological dig. No detail is too small to notice, and the accumulation of these little details can lead to larger patterns and instructional takeaways. You are building a comprehensive vision of potential, so you need to be comprehensive in your analysis. For math, this might have to do with the organization of the work or the sophistication of strategies. For writing, this could mean the mastery of sentence formation, invented versus standard spelling, and the development of ideas. A student's reading involves the ability to decode our alphabetic systems as well as orally discuss a text by using inferences and drawing conclusions. Figure 3.1 describes the process Mr. Matthews uses in his 2nd grade classroom.

You may wonder why teachers should begin by analyzing student work, especially student work that does not necessarily belong to the children they teach. You may also wonder why we should bother looking at student work from the grade above, especially if you have students who are struggling to achieve the goals from a previous grade. These concerns are fair, especially since teaching a wide range of students is one of the most profound challenges of classroom teaching. But in order to serve a spectrum of students, we need to prepare by studying a spectrum of possible student work. Despite our efforts to create grade-level standards and define grade-level work by age, we know students come into our classrooms with different levels of preparation. We need to know what great, high-quality work looks like along a spectrum so we can help our students grow and progress. The goal is to avoid stagnation in our instruction so students can make consistent progress and grow their skills—and this goal applies to *all* of our students.

FIGURE 3.1

Analyzing Exemplars in an ELA Class

Mr. Matthews's 2nd Grade ELA Class

Mr. Matthews is preparing to teach a 2nd grade ELA unit. By the end of the unit, students are expected to plan and write an informational paragraph based on research they conducted with a partner. Although the published unit came with an exemplar of student work, he isn't sure if it aligns with the goals for his class. To anchor his vision for student work, he seeks out exemplars of paragraph writing for 2nd and 3rd grade. After consulting online resources as well as student work available in his school and in the curriculum, Mr. Matthews pulls a few examples from 1st through 3rd grade.

Before he starts making a checklist of characteristics, Mr. Matthews notes the differences between the 2nd grade and 1st grade writing samples. What does the 2nd grader do that the 1st grader doesn't? Although the 1st grader wrote quite a few sentences, they do not center around one clear main idea like in the 2nd grade sample. This type of distinction matters. It is a kernel that can lead to high-leverage feedback and targeted teacher modeling. That feedback and modeling could be the difference between a student producing 2nd grade–quality work and 1st grade–quality work. Mr. Matthews notes the characteristics that distinguish the more advanced example.

After carefully reading each sample, he rereads them with different lenses. On his first reread, he notes the mastery of writing mechanics and conventions:

- Consistent capitalization at the starts of sentences, names, and places
- Consistent ending punctuation that matches the type of the sentence
- In the handwritten samples, correct letter formation that is easy to read and understand
- Few spelling errors except for multisyllable words that students may not know the rules for (e.g., *signiture* vs. *signature*)
- One or two small errors (which students can be taught to catch during the revision process)

On the next reread, Mr. Matthews looks for organization criteria:

- 1st grade sample is on topic, but details are not organized into clear subtopics
- 2nd grade paragraph has a topic sentence that introduces the main idea and relevant supporting details
- 3rd grade sample presents multiple paragraphs with organized subtopics and details

He then rereads the samples to identify precise writing choices that elevate the quality of the writing:

- Increase in sentence complexity with compound and complex sentences
- Correct use of past tense of verbs with some errors
- Final sentence that wraps up the paragraph or piece
- Title that matches the main idea of the paragraph or piece
- Variation in lengths and formats of sentences

Mr. Matthews's list may not be exhaustive, but he has enough to start creating a robust vision of what his students' work can look like. When he reviews the exemplar from the school's curriculum, he realizes that it mostly uses simple sentences, so he revises it to include more compound and complex sentence structures. He also creates a second exemplar with multiple paragraphs. He knows that, based on the exemplars, an informational paragraph is a reasonable goal for 2nd grade, but he also knows about 40 percent of his class could write multiple paragraphs with organized subtopics if provided the appropriate instruction, which is the 3rd grade goal. He is prepared to ensure all of his students meet the grade-level goal and to increase rigor where necessary.

We also know that our expectations matter. Although elementary school students, especially those in early elementary school, enter classrooms with a range of preparation, most students will rise to the expectations of their teachers (Russo & Hopkins, 2019). In Singapore, students move much more quickly through mathematical content than established by U.S. state standards, and their least confident math students outperform the most confident students in the United States on international assessments (Loveless, 2015). Grade-level standards are a helpful starting place, but they do not paint a complete picture of student potential. Expanding our definition of possible and holding students to the highest of expectations can make all the difference between below-grade-level and grade-level results. Students may not always fully meet the vision of their teacher, but they will go further and accomplish more when goals are ambitious. In the words of education author and consultant Tom Sherrington (2021):

> Nobody would think they have low expectations of students but I regularly observe that some teachers have much higher expectations than others. They create a more intense sense of purpose; they're that bit more bothered about standards of behaviour, talk, writing; they insist on accuracy and detail and don't accept mediocrity; they're more demanding of students in terms of their effort and general work load. They drive lessons with an energy that says "you can achieve, you can succeed; you can improve; you can do better." There's a sense of belief. (para. 4)

Teacher expectations are essential to student success, and there is much more risk in setting our goals too low than too high. Figure 3.2 depicts how Ms. Pierre embeds high expectations and a commitment to ambitious outcomes when she creates and analyzes math exemplars.

Make the Vision Concrete

Mr. Matthews and Ms. Pierre took their first step toward their visions by consulting student work (and state standards in the case of Ms. Pierre) to create an ambitious vision for academic achievement in their classrooms. By making checklists of particular characteristics, they gained clarity about not only what students *are* expected to do but also what students *can be* expected to do. Mr. Matthews realizes the original unit goal of informational paragraph writing should be the floor rather than the ceiling for his students, while Ms. Pierre ratcheted up the rigor of the teacher-created plans she inherited. What they are expecting of their students is much higher than if they continued relying on the materials they were initially given.

FIGURE 3.2

Analyzing Student Work and Creating Checklists for a Math Class

Ms. Pierre's 3rd Grade Math Class

Ms. Pierre is preparing to teach her students a fractions unit. Her school does not have a math curriculum, so she consults the Common Core State Standards (3.NF.1–3):

1. Understand a fraction $1/b$ as the quantity formed by 1 part when a whole is partitioned into b equal parts; understand a fraction a/b as the quantity formed by a parts of size $1/b$.
2. Understand a fraction as a number on the number line; represent fractions on a number line diagram.
3. Explain equivalence of fractions in special cases, and compare fractions by reasoning about their size.

The teacher-created lessons from past years are disjointed, and many are not aligned to the standards. Ms. Pierre therefore collects examples of 2nd, 3rd, and 4th grade fractions work to see the trajectory of instruction. She also downloads released questions from recent high-stakes tests in Massachusetts (www.doe.mass.edu/mcas/student/2022/grade3/math.html) and New York (www.nysedregents.org/ei/ei-math.html). After consulting these materials and an open-source math curriculum, Ms. Pierre creates an assessment aligned to the three fractions standards above. She then takes the assessment herself, using the strategies and representations required by the state standards, and generates a checklist of characteristics for each standard that her students will need to demonstrate.

1. Understand a fraction $1/b$ as the quantity formed by 1 part when a whole is partitioned into b equal parts; understand a fraction a/b as the quantity formed by a parts of size $1/b$.

- Students explain that a fraction is created when a whole is partitioned into equal parts.
- Each equal part can be represented as $1/b$, where b stands for the number of parts.
- You can count the fractional parts to make the whole, like "$1/3, 2/3, 3/3$."
- In past grades, students have learned about halves, quarters, and thirds. In 3rd grade, they also learn about sixths and eighths. Even though they may only focus on these types of fractions, they'll understand any whole can be divided into any number of equal parts.

2. Understand a fraction as a number on the number line; represent fractions on a number line diagram.

- In past grades, students mostly partitioned shapes like rectangles, circles, and hexagons. Now, they can look at a number line and divide the spaces between whole numbers.
- They can tick off equal parts (2, 3, 4, 6, 8) to represent $1/2, 2/2$, or $3/2$.
- They can count by fractions beyond whole numbers on the number line, for example, "One half, two halves, three halves." They can label these parts correctly on the number line as $1/2, 2/2, 3/2$. This will be a critical understanding for 4th grade, when students need to generate different equivalent fractions, so students will need to be able to count fractional parts beyond one whole.

(continued)

FIGURE 3.2 *continued*

Analyzing Student Work and Creating Checklists for a Math Class

> **3. Explain equivalence of fractions in special cases, and compare fractions by reasoning about their size.**
> • Students create visual models with shapes and number lines to show equivalence between fractions.
> • When drawing visual models, students are careful to keep the wholes equal. Otherwise, they aren't comparing equivalent fractions.
> • Students see the connection between division and fractions.
>   - 4 is the same as $4/_1$ or $4 \div 1$.
>   - $4/_2$ is the same as 2, $4 \div 2$, or $1/_2$ 4 times.
> • Explain the equivalence between fractional parts, for example, $1/_2$ is the same as $2/_4$.
>
> When Ms. Pierre looks at the 4th grade standards, she realizes how critical it is for her students to grasp the concept of equivalent fractions in 3rd grade. She plans ways to build fluency with counting as well as multiplication and division so that her students can meet and exceed the standards by the time they reach 4th grade.

Before continuing, I want to mention that the experiences of Mr. Matthews and Ms. Pierre often happen within the contexts of teams. Grade-level teams work together to look at student work and internalize the content they will teach. Some schools call this an "intellectual preparation protocol"; others call it "unpacking." In team settings, teachers can collaborate and do similar work to Mr. Matthews and Ms. Pierre.

But even with this excellent initial work, there is more to do. Now that Mr. Matthews and Ms. Pierre have a vision for student outcomes—what students should be able to say and do—the real challenge begins: how do they get students to an ambitious destination?

To begin with, schools and districts must prioritize the adoption of high-quality instructional materials so that educators are working with all the resources they need to best serve students. An ambitious vision for elementary students is not achievable without a rich and engaging curriculum. When we juxtapose the situations of Mr. Matthews and Ms. Pierre, we can clearly see that Ms. Pierre faces far more challenges to developing her ambitious plan than Mr. Matthews. Though no curriculum is perfect, Mr. Matthews already uses high-quality instructional materials, so he has much less to do.

Even so, investing in curriculum is no guarantee that the curriculum, especially a literacy curriculum, will build the knowledge students need to be successful. In a perfect school with perfect materials, the curriculum would consistently build and reinforce knowledge over the course of several years. Students would experience a litany of opportunities to learn and integrate information from history, science, geography, math, and art. Teachers wouldn't have to make additional efforts to supplement and revise the curriculum because the K–5, K–8, and perhaps even K–12, vertical alignment would be tight and clear.

Alas, these are not the present circumstances for a large number of teachers and schools. As practitioners, we need to be critical consumers of our curriculum materials, with a keen sense for what is purposeful and what is missing. This involves, first and foremost, teachers honing their content expertise. Similar to the process of analyzing exemplary student work, we need to take pride in building expertise in the content we teach. Perhaps it seems trivial to carefully think about the ways children add and subtract small numbers, but in the practice of that knowledge a teacher may uncover the crux of a child's understanding or misunderstanding. Careful reading of the texts in a scripted curriculum can reveal when students need specific vocabulary instruction or familiarity with particular topics before engaging with unit texts. Needless to say, teachers themselves should know the names of the continents and oceans before teaching students the names and locations of these places.

More and more, textbook companies market their curriculums as "knowledge-rich" in response to the body of research on knowledge and expertise. I have often found "knowledge-rich" curricula to have a lot of helpful materials, but they are rarely perfect. The best units can be taught with little revision, while others need significant attention. Teachers and building administrators still need to be the ultimate arbiters of curriculum and lesson quality. No scripted curriculum will ever fully take the place of a capable and knowledgeable teacher. This is the exact circumstance 2nd grade teacher Mr. Matthews finds himself in—needing to evaluate and adjust a high-quality curriculum to address his students' needs more appropriately.

The proliferation of free, open-source curricula available on the internet is a boon for teachers like Ms. Pierre. Her work setting a clear vision for student goals and outcomes will help her review her inherited folder of cobbled-together resources and suss out what she needs to keep, revise, remake, and reject.

Mr. Matthews and Ms. Pierre share the same next steps to make their ambitious visions concrete so they can execute them with students:

1. Define the specific domain knowledge kids will learn.
2. Determine what kids already know and fill in the gaps of what they need to know.

Define Specific Domain Knowledge

Whether working from an established curriculum or building a curriculum themselves, teachers will need to apply similar thinking processes. Defining specific domain knowledge means being crystal clear on what will be taught in a unit as well as anticipating common misconceptions.

Start with the learning goals in the curriculum. What will kids specifically need to do? Concisely summarize a text? Perform double-digit subtraction with regrouping? Describe the reasons for the Revolutionary War? These learning goals may come from the exemplar and standards analysis detailed above, or they may simply come from the school's prescribed curriculum. Even when using a prescribed curriculum, teachers may need to adjust some goals based on their preliminary work.

Make a list of knowledge taught in the given unit/module. What will kids need to know to meet the learning goals? For all subjects, you should look at the curriculum assessments and *take the tests*. When teachers perform the tasks they are asking of students, they can create a concrete artifact of their ambitious vision. Teachers can then determine what exactly student work will look like according to their vision. For ELA, teachers will need to read all the texts for a given unit and do the writing that students will be asked to do. In math, teachers should complete the problems in the final assessment.

After teachers do the student work, they can move into breaking down the knowledge and skills for the unit. One of the best ways to do this is by creating a What/How/Oops (WHO) chart (see Figure 3.3). What do students need to know? How will they show their learning? What could go wrong? How might they misunderstand the material? Figures 3.4 and 3.5 illustrate WHO charts for Mr. Matthews's and Ms. Pierre's classrooms.

FIGURE 3.3

What/How/Oops Chart

WHAT are they learning?	HOW will they demonstrate their learning?	OOPS—what could go wrong?
List what students are learning (e.g., specific concepts and vocabulary).	Identify how students will demonstrate their understanding (e.g., specific actions students will take).	What misunderstandings might students have? What will it sound like or look like when a student makes an error? (This list will grow the more you teach this particular content.)

Determine What Students Already Know and Still Need to Know

Identify prerequisite knowledge. What vocabulary, historical context, procedures, and strategies will students need to know to access the content? Even teachers with a robust unit plan or a detailed What/How/Oops chart won't get very far if students don't have the prerequisite knowledge to access the new material. One of the ways teachers can support deeper processing is by helping students integrate new knowledge with prior knowledge. Unfortunately, students may not have prior knowledge in the first place. Teachers need to define exactly what students need to know before the lesson and then determine if students have this prior knowledge.

Assess for prerequisites. It is crucial for teachers to know the students they are teaching. Teams can work collaboratively across grades to build vertical alignment so that there is a clear trajectory across the years. In the absence of that kind of alignment, teachers can look at the curriculum from past years. Of course, every teacher knows exposure to curriculum does not guarantee a student learned and retained the content taught. Teachers can use diagnostic assessments at the beginning of the year as well as pre-assessments at the start of units to evaluate what students already know. Chapter 5 will delve more into assessment planning.

FIGURE 3.4

WHO Charts for an ELA Class

Mr. Matthews's 2nd Grade ELA Class

Mr. Matthews knows what is possible for writing in his class, but he also needs to think about the other content students will be learning and writing about. In this unit, students are researching landforms and their impact on communities. Mr. Matthews generates two What/How/Oops charts for each of the unit's goals, one for writing and another for content. Mr. Matthews also refers to his exemplar student work checklist and the school's curriculum to help him fill out the chart.

Goal 1: Students will write an informational paragraph.

WHAT are they learning?	*HOW* will they demonstrate their learning?	*OOPS*—what could go wrong?
Informational writing—a genre where the author is informing the reader about a specific, nonfiction topic. **Topic sentence**—the first sentence that introduces the main idea of the paragraph. **Supporting details**—the specific examples that show the main idea and deepen the reader's understanding of the topic. **Conclusion**—a sentence that wraps up the paragraph and usually refers to the main idea again in a new way. **Capitalization conventions**—the rules for when a capital versus a lowercase letter is used in writing.	Students will **plan** their writing with a paragraph outline. It's OK if the plan doesn't have complete sentences or correct conventions. After planning their writing with an outline, students will **write** a paragraph with complete sentences. Once they are done with their first draft, students will **edit** and **revise** their paragraph. They will check that each sentence is complete, correct capitalization conventions are used, and the paragraph includes all required components.	Student omits one of the parts of a paragraph. Student selects supporting details that do not match the main idea. Student selects supporting details that match the main idea, but they are not the strongest examples based on the texts. Student writes in fragments, not complete sentences. Student confuses capitalization rules by capitalizing all nouns, not just proper nouns (e.g., "The Cat named Dotty is sleeping on the Couch").

Goal 2: Students will describe physical landforms and how communities develop around specific landforms.

WHAT are they learning?	*HOW* will they demonstrate their learning?	*OOPS*—what could go wrong?
Sea level—the height from where the ocean is. Imagine sea level is the 0 on a ruler. Everything taller than the ocean is above sea level, or higher than 0. **Elevation**—how high something is. **Mountains**—high-elevation landforms that are 1,000 feet tall or more. **Hills**—high-elevation landforms that are smaller than mountains; they are usually less than 1,000 feet tall. **Plateaus**—high-elevation landforms that are flat. **Plains**—flat areas at a low elevation. **Islands**—smaller pieces of land surrounded on all sides by water. **Rivers**—water, usually freshwater, that flows downhill. **Community**—a group of people who live together or regularly gather.	Students will **match** pictures of types of landforms with their definition. Students will **read** grade-level texts about landforms and communities around landforms, and **answer questions** about the texts (e.g., "How does the landform influence the community's way of life?" "Compare and contrast two communities and their landforms. How are their ways of life similar? How are they different?"). When answering questions about landforms and communities, students will **make explicit connections** between the landform and the community's architecture (how buildings are constructed), the way a community accesses resources, and transportation in a community.	Student confuses mountains and hills. Student describes the way of life in a community but does not connect that way of life with the type of landform. Student describes the landform but does not connect that landform with how a community lives. When comparing and contrasting two communities, student only notes the similarities or only notes the differences.

FIGURE 3.5

WHO Charts for a Math Class

Ms. Pierre's 3rd Grade Math Class

Ms. Pierre breaks down each of the fractions standards into a What/How/Oops chart. She refers to the checklist of characteristics she developed to complete the What and How categories.

3.NF.1. Understand a fraction 1/b as the quantity formed by 1 part when a whole is partitioned into b equal parts; understand a fraction a/b as the quantity formed by a parts of size 1/b.

WHAT are they learning?	*HOW* will they demonstrate their learning?	*OOPS*—what could go wrong?
Unit fraction—when a whole is equally divided into parts, each part is represented as 1/b. For example, when a whole is divided into three parts, each part represents $\frac{1}{3}$. **Numerator**—the number of fractional parts of a whole. This number goes on the top of the line in a fraction (e.g., the 1 in $\frac{1}{5}$). **Denominator**—the number of parts a whole has been divided into. This number goes on the bottom of the line in a fraction (e.g., the 5 in $\frac{1}{5}$).	Given a shape, such as a rectangle or circle or line, students will **divide** the shape into equal parts. Students will represent each fractional part as 1/b. Students will **count the parts** of the fraction (e.g., given a rectangle divided into fifths, students count each of the parts as $\frac{1}{5}, \frac{2}{5}, \frac{3}{5}, \frac{4}{5}, \frac{5}{5}$). Students will **explain** that when all the parts are counted together, they equal the whole.	Student does not equally divide a shape. Student confuses the numerator and denominator (e.g., for a shape partitioned into fifths, student represents each part as $\frac{5}{1}$). Student treats $\frac{5}{5}$ as a different amount from 1 whole.

3.NF.2. Understand a fraction as a number on the number line; represent fractions on a number line diagram.

WHAT are they learning?	HOW will they demonstrate their learning?	OOPS—what could go wrong?
Number line—each number on the number line represents one whole.	Students will **equally divide one whole** on a number line into fractional parts. Students will **divide more than one whole** into fractional parts. Dividing up to the number 2 on the number line means two wholes were divided. When dividing more than one whole number into fractional parts, students will **count** each of those fractional parts, even beyond one whole (e.g., $\frac{1}{4}$, $\frac{2}{4}$, $\frac{3}{4}$, $\frac{4}{4}$, $\frac{5}{4}$, $\frac{6}{4}$, $\frac{7}{4}$).	Student treats whole numbers on a number line as part of the fraction rather than as a divided whole (e.g., $\frac{1}{1}$, $\frac{2}{1}$, $\frac{3}{1}$; $\frac{1}{2}$, $\frac{2}{2}$, $\frac{3}{2}$). When dividing more than one whole number on the number line into fourths, student treats multiple wholes as one whole (e.g., dividing numbers from 0 to 2 into four parts instead of eight).

3.NF.3. Explain equivalence of fractions in special cases, and compare fractions by reasoning about their size.

WHAT are they learning?	HOW will they demonstrate their learning?	OOPS—what could go wrong?
Equivalent—equal in value. **Equivalent fractions**—fractions with the same value even though the whole was divided into a different number of parts.	Students will **create visual models** of fractions to compare their size. • On two number lines of the same size, students will represent both fractions to see if they are the same size. • Using two shapes of the same size, students will partition both shapes into fractional parts and compare sizes to see if the fractions are equivalent.	Student creates a model but the number lines or shapes are not the same size.

Teach to fill knowledge gaps without disrupting grade-level instruction. Teachers can embed missing prerequisite knowledge into short mini-lessons, quick reviews at the beginning of class, small-group interventions, and other brief opportunities during the school day. For instance, 3rd graders struggling with prefixes and suffixes learned in 2nd grade can review them during a morning meeting message, or the teacher can lead a quick choral response review during the first few minutes of the ELA lesson. Students with weaker addition and subtraction skills can complete morning work aligned with those gaps during the arrival period, or teachers can provide them with flash cards to review during transitions and quiet periods of the day. If the whole class is struggling with skip-counting forward and backward, every transition is the opportunity to practice. Students can practice while walking to and from the classroom rug, lining up for lunch and recess, and even as an activity when a lesson finishes early. More examples of how to address missing prerequisites appear in Chapter 6.

Of course, some students will struggle more than others. Teachers may need to use the school's learning specialists and Response to Intervention (RTI) program to truly support every student. However, teachers should not assume right away that a student is too "low achieving" or "behind" to access grade-level content. See Figures 3.6 and 3.7 for how Mr. Matthews and Ms. Pierre work to help their students close gaps in understanding. Substantially altering student work expectations should occur only after a number of strategic interventions have been tried. We have to be careful not to exclude students from our ambitious vision simply because they need some additional support.

Conclusion

Few teachers possess the mental bandwidth or time to craft brand-new units with unique essential questions, lessons, and student-facing materials. Yet we should never capitulate to a false yet too often promulgated avowal that teaching, especially the teaching of young children, is easy, because students need only to be told 2 + 2 = 4 and this letter makes this sound in order to succeed. Most teachers and administrators do not promote this shallow definition of teaching; however, every year, schools and school districts invest gargantuan

FIGURE 3.6

Closing Gaps in an ELA Class

Mr. Matthews's 2nd Grade ELA Class

Mr. Matthews's curriculum relies on students possessing a number of prerequisite skills and knowledge to fully access and understand the new material. They will not only need to know the vocabulary taught in the unit but also some basic geography. The texts are set in different countries and regions, so students will at the very least need to know the names of Earth's seven continents and five oceans.

Even though his students received writing instruction in 1st grade, Mr. Matthews knows from experience that incoming 2nd graders often still struggle with the basics of writing. To write paragraphs successfully, they will need to have a command of basic sentence writing and to know the difference between a sentence fragment and a complete sentence.

In preparation for the unit, Mr. Matthews teaches short lessons on the names and locations of the continents and oceans. He posts a map in the classroom for the students to refer to. At least once a week, he gives the students a pop quiz or conducts a five-minute review. He does not roll out paragraph writing right away, but instead starts every class with a sentence activity where students distinguish between sentence fragments and complete sentences, even in non-ELA instruction periods such as math or science.

FIGURE 3.7

Closing Gaps in a Math Class

Ms. Pierre's 3rd Grade Math Class

When Ms. Pierre looks at the fractions work students did previously in 1st and 2nd grade, she realizes most of her students have only worked with partitioning two-dimensional shapes into halves, fourths, and thirds. In 3rd grade, students will also be dividing shapes and number lines into fifths, sixths, and eighths. She wants to make sure that students understand a whole can be divided into any number of equal parts, even though they may only be familiar with certain common fractions.

Ms. Pierre also considers what students will need to understand about the word *equivalence*. According to the Common Core Standards, students in 1st grade should have learned about the meaning of the equal sign. Two different expressions can be equal, such as $5 + 10 = 20 - 5$. Based on her own experience with her school's disjointed curriculum, Ms. Pierre anticipates her students may have entered 3rd grade with an inconsistent understanding of the equal sign, which could affect their understanding of equivalent fractions.

Ms. Pierre proactively plans with these prerequisites in mind. She decides to implement a lesson prior to the start of the unit to review what a fraction is. She shows students many different examples of partitioning a shape or quantity into equal parts. During morning meeting, she gives students a "blast from the past" review problem, taking this time to review the meaning of the equal sign using addition and subtraction examples. After the review, she will show students examples of equivalent fractions using whole numbers before moving into equivalent fractional parts during the math lesson.

sums of money in instructional materials because they subscribe to a version of the idea: that with the right scripted lesson plans that tell teachers the precise words to say and the precise time to say them, students will learn all that they need to know. Unfortunately, the learning transaction between teacher and student is much more complex than that.

When teachers prepare to execute their school's curriculum, there is much to consider, as this chapter demonstrates; nevertheless, it is important to mine the curriculum for gold. Even with a decade of experience, I *never* wholly or even partially disregard quality curriculum materials provided to me. These materials make a real difference in my ability to make strategic decisions for my students. However, some curricula furnish teachers with 10- to 15-page lesson plans full of rich and interesting directions for a lesson, from extensive descriptions of teacher actions to exemplar student work. Despite authors' good intentions, a lengthy plan such as this can present its own challenge: teachers can't possibly enact every good idea (or revise every bad one) in a prescriptive curriculum. A teacher or teaching team approaching these materials can use the process outlined in this chapter to prune and build on a generic plan to make it into something rigorous, engaging, and, hopefully, transformational for students.

Chapter 3 Key Points

- Create an ambitious vision based on exemplary student work at and above grade level.

- Plan for how students will gain knowledge through units of study.

- Assess whether students have the necessary background knowledge for a new unit. Use all parts of the school day to close gaps in knowledge without disrupting grade-level instruction.

4 PLANNING FOR INSTRUCTION WITH THE CRITICAL THINKING FRAMEWORK

In my first year at a new school, I was tasked with teaching the 3rd grade ELA curriculum. Like many teachers, there were things I liked in the curriculum and things I didn't, but for the most part, I executed the lessons with fidelity. And then we got to *Peter Pan.*

The 3rd grade curriculum included an adapted version of the original J. M. Barrie novel, which students read over the course of several weeks. While the unit included a short article explaining some of the historical context of late 19th century Great Britain, I found myself horrified while rereading the book. Students were expected to skim over blatant stereotypes about gender roles and American Indians to identify character traits and answer text-dependent questions with evidence. Moreover, the unit left out crucial vocabulary and content knowledge that would help students access the plot and characteristics of the fantasy genre. Despite my displeasure, 30 hardcover books waited in a large drawer. Replacing the text was not an option.

I decided to reframe the unit. I obeyed the pacing calendar and read Chapter 2 on Tuesday and Chapter 3 on Wednesday, but I deliberately adjusted my questions and materials so students could critically unpack the messages in the book. (I worked at a school that encouraged teachers to modify curriculum to make it more culturally responsive.) I knew students could not engage in this kind of thinking work unless they had the required content knowledge. In addition to reading the book, I taught minilessons on cultural biases in early 20th century Great Britain. We defined the word *stereotype* and discussed places we encounter stereotypes already, such as in toy ads. As we read, students annotated their books with sticky notes when they noticed a stereotype. They made explicit connections to the historical context of late 19th century Britain, which helped us unpack the ways characters like Wendy and the Lost Boys were presented differently. After finishing the book, we watched videos and read articles about the inaccurate representations of American Indians in our current media and recent history. Students left the unit not only equipped to analyze a fantasy text but also possessing an expanded base of *knowledge.*

Students then had a choice—they either wrote a letter to the principal about whether they thought we should continue reading *Peter Pan* in 3rd grade, or they wrote a letter to author J. M. Barrie with feedback on his novel (these tasks followed lessons on the structure of a letter and how to plan a persuasive argument). Some may assume that every student argued that 3rd graders shouldn't read the book—that my decision to teach students to critically evaluate this text amounted to proselytizing a specific worldview. Much to the contrary, the 3rd graders expressed surprisingly nuanced opinions. Some came to the conclusion that *Peter Pan* should be read by older students but not younger students, who might not comprehend some of the misleading representations. Other students felt strongly that 3rd graders should keep reading the book so that kids could learn to recognize and call out stereotypes, but that they should read a book right afterward that didn't have those problems. Still others loved the book for its adventure and jokes, arguing that the book's fun-loving spirit more than made up for its deficits. And a few more thought that the book was too old-fashioned and that other, newer books should be read instead.

As described in earlier chapters, I used my ambitious vision to further challenge my students. The students still learned how to identify character traits and respond to text-dependent questions with evidence. But they also learned how to critically read, analyze, and evaluate a text in a way that superseded the rigor of the original unit. The tasks in the original unit asked students to write a paragraph, and in the end they composed multiparagraph essays. The unit also asked students to revise a scene from the book, but instead, the 3rd graders created their own fantasy tales, some of which told a story over several chapters. My colleague and coteacher even taught lessons on common tropes and stereotypes within the fantasy and fairy tale genres, which helped students reflect on their own stories.

Most teachers are handed a curriculum and told to teach it. This can be frustrating, especially when we encounter dry, boring texts and activities where students are never given necessary content knowledge or the opportunity to process big ideas. Perhaps worse, we sometimes find we are handed texts and materials that promote and reinforce racist and sexist ideas. Sometimes we can advocate to change these materials, but sometimes our hands are tied due to budgets or intractable school politics. So what can we do?

Teachers possess more power in their classrooms than the systems they work within would suggest. Schools and districts often exclude teachers from important policy decisions, such as choosing a curriculum or setting a reform agenda, but teachers are in their classrooms day after day making millions of decisions beyond the purview of an administrator's office. Teachers need an approach to mandated curriculum that helps them be critical consumers of products that vary in quality and usefulness. When executing prescriptive curriculum, we can make decisions to elevate the instructional expectations and classroom experiences for our children.

In Chapter 3, I discussed how teachers can make informed adjustments to a set curriculum based on an ambitious vision of student achievement. Now our focus narrows to instructional planning on the lesson level as we address three common pitfalls that undermine knowledge building and deep processing. By the end of this chapter, you will walk away with concrete strategies to avoid these pitfalls and design high-impact lessons.

The "In One Ear, Out the Other" Problem

It's all well and good to talk about knowledge and ambitious goals and share anecdotes like mine about *Peter Pan*. But some readers, especially newer teachers, might be thinking something like, "I'm happy that you can do it, but when I teach my kids information, everything goes in one ear and out the other. I could tell my students about the characteristics of fantasy and 19th century gender roles in Great Britain, but my students will just forget it."

And the truth is, that's probably what is happening. It is insufficient to know the knowledge and skills you want students to master without knowing how to help them independently remember and do the things they are being taught. A few reasons likely account for why your lessons feel like pouring water through a colander:

- Students are processing information in a shallow way.

- Lessons are presented in such a way that student working memory is overwhelmed.

- Only some, not all, students are being asked to engage in the thinking work of a lesson.

This list is not exhaustive, but during my teaching career, these three factors represent the most persistent problems undermining high-quality lesson execution. If we are dedicated to educating critical thinkers, we need to address these common pitfalls.

Shallow Information Processing

Even when teachers work tirelessly to create engaging lessons for students, high engagement does not guarantee students will retain learning. How well we remember something has to do with how we process that information. As teachers, we need to consider whether our lessons foster shallow or deep processing.

What's the difference?

Let's say I'm teaching a brand-new vocabulary word to my students. We are in the midst of a unit on fossils, and we are going to learn the word *petrified*. I could ask students to look at the word and notice the size of the letters, the font type, or even the colors. I could also have the students clap the syllables (*pet-ri-fied*), count the number of letters, or trace the word with their fingers. I could create a song with the word and definition that students sing again and again. All of these activities are fun and memorable for students, but if my goal is for students to remember the word, understand its meaning, and recognize it in a text, then I need to help students process the word in a way that emphasizes its meaning. That requires students to know not only the definition but also how to apply it in different contexts.

I don't need to ditch the fun song or the spelling exercises, but these activities alone are insufficient. Rather than processing the physical or sensory features of a word, students should look for semantic (i.e., meaning-based) connections. In other words, they should make connections between the word and past experiences and knowledge. Recall our discussion of the word *spring* in Chapter 1. Every time we encounter the word *spring*, either in a text or through instruction, we connect the word in the current context to previous contexts. This process of making meaning by linking to prior knowledge leads to better memory retention. Semantic connections are also relevant to our earlier discussion of novices and experts. Experts, like chess masters, demonstrate their wider and more effective memories through semantic processing of chessboards. When they analyze chessboards to remember them, they are attending to the relationships between the pieces, the type of game and strategy employed, and the associations with prior chess match experiences. Novices simply do not have the same amount of information stored in long-term memory, so they are more limited in the kind of processing they do.

In the example of *petrified,* students may learn physical features of the word, like how it is spelled, or phonemic features (how it is pronounced), but they must have an opportunity to integrate the concept of *petrified* with their prior knowledge. When introducing the word, a teacher might explain that the word *petrification* describes a step in the fossilization process. After an organism dies and its body decays, hard parts, like bones and teeth, can become *petrified,* or turned to stone. Students can sort pictures or compare and contrast petrified fossils with fossils found in amber or ice. These types of activities ask students to engage in deeper processing by focusing on conceptual meaning.

Of course, students may not have any prior knowledge. As discussed in Chapter 3, our high-level planning of units and lessons has to account for gaps in prior knowledge. If we know students won't be able to make a connection to a concept, we have to plan to teach them. We can't assume students will just be able to "pick it up" somehow or research unfamiliar topics on their own. We have to use the resources of the classroom to provide the necessary background knowledge efficiently and clearly so that deep, semantic processing can happen.

Don't misunderstand—the goal of deeper processing is not just helping kids memorize content more effectively. If anything, deep processing requires teachers to better understand the role that meaning making plays in memory. Integrating new learning with prior knowledge is an active process. Students will need to do something with their learning through discussion, writing, or practice. To learn and retain factual knowledge such as multiplication tables and the names of capitals, they must apply it.

Overwhelmed Working Memory

Lessons can implode for a number of reasons. Students become confused, lost, or "out to lunch," and teachers are left wondering what they could have done differently. Often, student confusion has to do with two things: a lack of prior knowledge and an unclear presentation of the information or task. Both of these issues are connected to working memory.

Working memory refers to the information that can be held in mind while engaged in a cognitive task. Chapter 1 discussed how working memory is finite—it can only hold a few items at a time. Every teacher in every lesson is engaging the working memories of their students. Understanding how working memory functions can help you make thoughtful instructional choices. Despite the attractive claims of different programs, there is no evidence that you can increase your working memory or the working memory of students.

So why does it seem like some people can hold a lot more in their head at once than others? Some of it may be a difference in working memory capacity, though in most circumstances, this difference depends on the content being thought about. The more relevant information stored in long-term memory is, the more effectively you can think about a topic in the moment. (See the discussion of schemata in Chapter 1.) Oftentimes, classrooms ask students to learn new content even when they don't possess the prerequisite information in their long-term memory. Their working memory, overloaded by all the new information, cannot engage in deep processing. Information stored in long-term memory is the difference between Harry, the experienced bread baker we met in Chapter 1, and Phoebe, the novice floundering through her first recipe.

It's crucial for teachers to chunk the content they are teaching. In the words of education psychologist Barak Rosenshine (2010), "present new material using small steps" (p. 10). I know from personal experience that teachers often feel a strong urge to jump into the hardest question and task right away. For our most prepared students, this may feel like a worthwhile challenge. But for many students, competence must precede confidence. They need to first shore up their prerequisite skills so they can take on challenges. Kids know when teachers have set them up to fail, and it isn't a good feeling. When they are given the tools they need in a clear and careful progression, kids will be more open to risks and moments of failure. We want Phoebe the novice to try again, not to throw away her book.

Few Students Engaging in Thinking Work

In most classrooms, participation is determined by volunteers raising their hands. Volunteerism is comfortable—the students who are comfortable speaking, usually the most extroverted and confident students, share their thinking with the class. However, volunteerism leads to a number of problematic outcomes: teachers fail to notice trends of understanding and misunderstanding in their classroom; quieter, less confident students are ignored; and students who are on the cusp of understanding do not get the opportunity to engage in deep processing, which we know is integral to retaining new learning.

Every student needs an opportunity to respond to questions throughout a lesson. The ability to frequently respond to questions about content is connected to deeper learning and retention (MacSuga-Gage & Simonsen, 2015). In what are sometimes called *total participation techniques*, every student is asked to respond to the teacher's questions—no opting out. This ensures that every single student is engaged in the thinking so the teacher can monitor everyone. These techniques fall into the bucket of what some call "formative assessment," but they go a step further than just asking everyone a question. Total participation techniques are protocols and activities where no student is left out. Total participation is an essential component of practice for teachers who care deeply about equitable outcomes for all their students.

Some may balk at the requirements of total participation techniques, such as asking every student to write on a whiteboard or consider a question before a cold call. In classrooms where students do not feel safe and secure in making mistakes, total participation techniques can feel more like a punishment than a productive routine. I will address this concern in Chapter 7, but for now, I encourage you to consider the following points:

- When we call on only a few students, we communicate to the entire class which students we consider worthy of attention. Often the most confident, fastest processing students will be given a tacit rank within the classroom. Even if we don't intend to, we can cause some students to start to believe the thoughts and ideas of some matter more than others. This perception occurs even in the youngest grades.

- When we do not ask every student to respond to our questions, we risk creating a false positive when monitoring for understanding. If we monitor the highest achieving students, we might assume a level of understanding not representative of the class as a whole.

Avoiding the Pitfalls

When planning a lesson, we learn to start with an objective and then plan instructional activities to enable students to master the objective (backward planning). Some schools follow the I-We-You model for planning, in which the teacher explicitly introduces an objective, models the skill, guides student practice, and then gives students a chance to demonstrate their learning. Others use an inverted constructivist model, where students first attempt to solve a problem without instruction. The teacher then introduces the skill or facilitates a discussion where students put together key components of the skill.

Strong opinions exist about which one of these two models (or any of their many permutations) more effectively supports student learning. No matter which model you prefer, the pitfalls described above come into play. Shallow processing, overwhelmed working memories, and inequitable student participation will plague lessons that haven't been planned to avoid such negative impacts.

Let's look at three types of instruction planning using the Critical Thinking Framework: meaning-making activities, teacher-led discussions, and total participation techniques.

Meaning-Making Activities

All lessons include activities, but not all activities ensure students engage in deep processing, nor do they ensure students can engage in the lesson without their working memories becoming overwhelmed. As cognitive scientist Daniel Willingham (2009) wrote in *Why Don't Students Like School?* "whatever students think about is what they will remember" (p. 54). Deceptively simple, this statement is not always heeded while planning instruction; it certainly did not inform decisions I made early in my career.

In a 2nd grade unit on fractions, I scoured the internet for a way to teach my students the standards. (Much like the school employing Chapter 3's Ms. Pierre, my school did not provide a curriculum.) At the time, I believed students would only learn the content I taught if it were fun, so I clicked on links to bright arts and crafts projects. I decided to teach my students how to make a "fraction robot." The activity involved cutting and gluing lots of construction paper, which took students almost the entirety of the block to complete. I spent most of the lesson carefully instructing students on how to keep their materials organized, accurately cut the pieces, and glue the robot together. At the end, students created an adorable craft, and their smiles made me declare immediate victory—a short-lived one. When I gave them a quiz on fractions the next day, they did not remember anything about the names of the fractions we had learned about or how to divide shapes into fractions.

I still believe in fun, and I would even go so far as to say fun should exist in schools for its own sake. But my attention to fun alone did not produce the learning I wanted. To return to Willingham's maxim, if students remember what they think about, my students probably remembered the organizing, cutting, and gluing that my lesson emphasized. My students probably thought a lot about what they were doing, but very little of that thinking involved fractions.

So how can teachers structure lessons to make meaning?

Let's apply lessons from the pitfalls described earlier. Based on the working memory pitfall, we know students will not retain learning if it is not presented in small enough steps. So first, the teacher needs to chunk the objectives into a manageable sequence. This work depends on whether the teacher adapts a prescriptive curriculum or creates their own. In the former instance, teachers may take provided lessons and break them apart as needed. Teachers who create their own lessons from scratch need to look at the amount of time scheduled for the lesson and determine what they can adequately address in that period. Much of this work can be done when teachers define the specific domain knowledge that kids will learn through a What/How/Oops chart (refer back to Figure 3.3).

Second, teachers need to select activities that require students to make meaning of the content. As we discussed, students make meaning by connecting new learning to prior knowledge and by engaging in tasks that ask them to think about the content. Here, the Critical Thinking Framework can help us think about the types of thinking tasks we can present to students to encourage deep processing.

To illustrate these two principles, let me indulge in every teacher's fantasy and enter an alternate universe where I can turn back time and repair a lesson gone wrong.

In this alternate reality, I am wary of using cute internet activities to teach content to students. I want to focus first on the content students need to know. I identify the grade-level fractions standards and create a What/How/Oops chart (see Figure 4.1).

With this WHO chart done, I can break the standard into smaller, more manageable objectives for my students:

- SWBAT [Students will be able to] describe how to equally partition circles and rectangles into two, three, and four equal shares by drawing their partitions and describing them as halves, thirds, and fourths.

- When presented with drawings of circles and rectangles divided into halves, thirds, and fourths with some parts shaded, SWBAT to describe the shapes as $2/3$, $3/4$, and so forth and represent the amount with a numerator and denominator.

- SWBAT reproduce fractions such as $2/3$ and $1/4$ using drawings of rectangles and circles and correctly shading the fractional parts.

- SWBAT describe how a shape may be partitioned in different shapes and the partitions will still be equal to one another.

FIGURE 4.1

WHO Chart for Fractions Lesson

Standard NY-2.G.3. Partition circles and rectangles into two, three, or four equal shares. Describe the shares using the words *halves, thirds, half of, a third of*, etc. Describe the whole as *two halves, three thirds, four fourths.* Recognize that equal shares of identical wholes need not have the same shape.

WHAT are they learning?	*HOW* will they demonstrate their learning?	*OOPS*—what could go wrong?
Halves—two equal shares. **Thirds**—three equal shares. **Fourths and quarters**—four equal shares. **Numerator**—the number above the line in a fraction that shows the number of shares. **Denominator**—the number below the line in a fraction that shows the total number of shares in one whole.	Students will divide circles and rectangles into equal shares. Students will say, "When I make thirds, I divide the shape into three equal pieces." Students will say, "When I make fourths, I divide the shape into four equal pieces." When partitioning the shape, students will ensure the parts are the same size and shape. When presented with shaded parts of a divided shape, students will describe it as "$2/3$." Students will shade in and represent fractions such as $3/4$ and $1/2$. Students will explain that a whole is the same as all the shares put together. For example, they will say, "The whole is the same as four fourths."	Student thinks there is only one correct way to partition shapes. For example, a square divided into four equal shares is the same as a square divided into four equal triangles if the wholes are the same. When dividing the shape, a student does not make sure all the shares are the same shape and size. Student looks at two rectangles divided into fourths in different ways and claims they are not equal. Student only describes part of the fraction. Instead of saying $2/3$, student says, "There are two pieces" or "There are thirds." Student flips the fraction and describes $3/4$ as $4/3$ ("four thirds"). Student treats $4/4$ and one whole as different amounts.

Now that the standard is chunked into smaller objectives, I can turn to the Critical Thinking Framework to help me plan meaning-making activities for students, being sure to anticipate the "Oops" section of my What/How/Oops chart (see Figure 4.2).

FIGURE 4.2

Planning Meaning-Making Activities for Fractions Lesson

Objective	Meaning-Making Activities
SWBAT describe how to equally partition circles and rectangles into two, three, and four equal shares by drawing their partitions and describing them as halves, thirds, and fourths.	After introducing the vocabulary (*halves, thirds, fourths*), I present students with a series of examples and nonexamples of partitioned shapes. I ask students to **notice the gaps and inconsistencies** as well as **say in their own words** how they know one example is equally partitioned and another is not. When students practice partitioning their own shapes, either as a drawing or with a tactile material like play dough, I ask them to **break down** their process and explain to me the steps they're taking.
When presented with drawings of circles and rectangles divided into halves, thirds, and fourths with some parts shaded, SWBAT to describe the shapes as $^2/_3$, $^3/_4$, and so forth and represent the amount with a numerator and denominator.	First, students learn the vocabulary for numerator and denominator before looking at representations of shaded fractional parts. Students are then presented with two circles, one representing $^1/_3$ and another $^2/_3$. They are asked to **look for structure** in the two examples by responding to the question "What is similar and different between these two examples?" Students connect to the knowledge developed earlier in the unit by noticing that both circles are divided into thirds. They then note, "In one circle, one of the thirds is shaded, and in the other, two of the thirds are shaded." Depending on the class and preferred lesson structure, I may ask students to try to represent the fractions with numerators and denominators, or I may model with this example and then have students practice with subsequent examples. After students engage in solid practice with representing the fractions until at least 75–80 percent of students are doing it correctly, they can continue to **look for structure** by answering questions such as "What if all three of my thirds are shaded in? How would I represent that amount?" Once they can describe the representation as $^3/_3$, ask, "How can I finish this sentence? Three thirds is the same as _____?" Help students see that $^3/_3$ is the same as one whole. They can also keep counting by thirds to describe amounts like $^4/_3$, $^5/_3$, etc.

Objective	Meaning-Making Activities
SWBAT reproduce fractions such as $2/3$ and $1/4$ using drawings of rectangles and circles and correctly shading the fractional parts.	At this point, students consolidate their understanding of halves, thirds, and fourths. In addition to producing drawings of fractions with rectangles and circles, they **notice the gaps and inconsistencies** in nonexamples. They can explain to a partner or in writing mistakes in a nonexample. The nonexamples address common misconceptions, like flipping the numerator and denominator, or not dividing the shape into equal shares in the first place. While students are doing this work, I require them to **say in their own words** what they are doing. Frequent explanations help students synthesize their learning and surface misconceptions. For instance, I may notice a student not using the vocabulary correctly. I prompt the student, saying, "Say it again, but this time instead of saying 'pieces,' say 'fourths.'"
SWBAT describe how a shape may be partitioned in different shapes and the partitions will still be equal to one another.	With this objective, I directly address a stubborn misunderstanding that students often express in early elementary school. Looking at a rectangle of the same size divided into fourths in different ways, students will say the fourths in the two rectangles are not equal. For students to comprehend that a shape of the same size can be divided into fourths in different ways and the fourths will still be equal, they need to analyze multiple examples. While analyzing the examples, students **look for structure** by responding to questions such as "What pattern do we notice?" and "What's a rule for the pattern we're seeing?"

I can step out of the alternate reality confident that my refreshed lesson would set my students up for a deeper learning experience. In my example, I used tools we learned about in Chapter 3 to break down what I want students to learn with the WHO chart and chunked the learning into smaller objectives and tasks. This process helped me avoid the pitfall of overwhelming my students with too much content at one time. I then used the Critical Thinking Framework to plan activities for each objective, which asked students to engage in deep processing of the learning. I avoided extraneous activities that could distract students from the content.

Embedded in Figure 4.2 are a number of questions to pose to students during discussion. Teacher-led discussions are a powerful way to elicit deeper processing of content.

Teacher-Led Discussions

In Abrami and colleagues' (2015) meta-analysis, the authors identify two instructional strategies that lead to development in critical thinking for students across grades K–12:

> Notably, the opportunity for dialogue (e.g., discussion) appears to improve the outcomes of CT [critical thinking] skills acquisition, especially where the teacher poses questions, when there are both whole-class teacher-led discussions and teacher-led group discussions. Similarly, the exposure of students to authentic or situated problems and examples seems to play an important role in promoting CT, particularly when applied problem solving and role-playing methods are used. (p. 302)

In these discussions, students are not simply producing rote memorization and regurgitation of facts and figures. They are engaged in teacher-directed activities that require consideration of questions, discussion, and application of what they are learning.

The meta-analysis also found large effect sizes when teacher-led discussions and problem solving are combined with mentoring (here defined as one-on-one tutoring, peer-led partnerships, and internships). Two-thirds of the studies supporting this finding were with college/postgraduate students, while one-third was with high school students. For this reason, we are not diving deeply into the mentorship component; however, it is important to note that mentoring seemed to contribute only in combination with discussion and problem solving, not when it was used as a stand-alone intervention.

Worthwhile Questions for Worthwhile Conversations

Although high-quality curricula may provide a number of thought-provoking questions and activities that promote dialogue, the onus ultimately rests with the teacher to foster meaningful student discourse. Teachers need a way to sort the good from the bad in scripted curricula, or a way to craft questions from scratch when they lack the resources they need from the start.

No worthwhile conversation is possible without a worthwhile question. The Critical Thinking Framework provides a foundation to create question stems that activate student thinking and encourage students to make meaning-based connections to prior learning.

Figure 4.3 presents question stems for each of the five components of the framework, which can be employed in all grades and at graduated levels of complexity. Once again, in the absence of content instruction, these question stems alone are insufficient to support student learning. They are only effective when they are paired with clearly presented information.

By posing thoughtful questions, we can invite students to think more deeply about the content they are learning, make connections to prior learning, and revise misconceptions. Questions aligned with the Critical Thinking Framework push students to analyze, evaluate, and construct judgments.

Often, teachers avoid class discussions for the very reason they are helpful to students: the possible surfacing of wrong answers and misconceptions. Rather than cast students saying the wrong thing as uncomfortable, we should welcome and embrace the opportunity. When misunderstandings come to the fore, we can leverage the whole-group discussion to address them.

The difference between a successful and unsuccessful discussion lies, as it does in so much of teaching, in the planning. Before facilitating a discussion with students, teachers need to plan their questions based on the lesson objective. In my alternative reality lesson, students consolidated the key points of fractions by critiquing examples and nonexamples of halves, thirds, and fourths. I then used my questions to address common misconceptions, such as flipping the numerator and denominator. As we saw in that example, when teachers predict misconceptions and common errors, they can proactively plan questions to clarify student understanding. Discussions and questions become a powerful tool. Chapter 6 digs further into how the Critical Thinking Framework can help teachers address student errors and misconceptions, with specific examples of teacher responses, some occurring in the context of teacher-led discussion.

While teacher-led discussions are powerful, they can still sometimes fall into the pitfall of only some, not all, students engaging in the thinking work of the lesson. Teachers need a repertoire of total participation techniques that equitably include the voices of all students in the lesson. Successful discussions integrate these techniques to avoid relying on volunteers alone.

FIGURE 4.3

Question Stems for the Critical Thinking Framework

Say it in your own words	Can you say it in your own words? The author said _____. What do they mean by that? Can you write a one-sentence summary of the passage? In one sentence, what is the big idea here? Explain what _____ just said in your own words.
Break it down	What is the first step? Next? Then? Why did they [insert step from procedure]? How does that make sense? What if I were to skip this part? What would happen? Why? Can I substitute _____ for _____? Why or why not?
Look for structure	What is the same and different between these two examples? Have we seen something like this before? Where? Why is it the same here? What pattern do we see here? Is there a rule that describes what we're talking about? Does _____ apply to all situations? When would I do _____ instead? When does the rule not apply? Give me an example and a nonexample.
Notice gaps and inconsistencies	Do you agree with _____? Why or why not? Can I try it this way? Will it still work? It sounds like _____ and _____ are making different points. Which do we agree with? Why? Compare _____ with _____. How are they similar and different? Look at this work sample. There are two things I can do right away to improve it. What are they?
Reason with evidence	What makes you think that? Can you put your finger on the word or sentence that shows _____? What word or phrase shows _____? Which piece of evidence is stronger? How do you know?

Total Participation Techniques

Learning structures that engage students in active listening, thinking, discussion, and response fuel understanding and critical thinking (Martin et al., 2018). If we think back to our definition of critical thinking, students need to use what they know to analyze, evaluate, and make judgments. It is impossible to do any of those things without ample opportunities for active learning. We also cannot expect the active participation of a few students to rub off on their peers. We must set the expectation of every student fully participating and having an opportunity to respond to our questions. Every student has to learn and be able to apply the material.

Sometimes teachers create false positives of student participation, asking questions such as "How confident do you feel about _____?" or "Thumbs up or thumbs down if you understand or not." These types of softball questions and activities often come from a place of empathy for students—they can make everyone feel part of the lesson. Unfortunately, this surface-level engagement produces a mirage of learning, not learning itself. At the lesson level, lessons need to be structured with total participation techniques that require all students to respond to questions *about the content.*

Examples of total participation techniques include the following:

- Whiteboards where every student shows their work

- Simultaneous voting (given a set of two to four options, students hold up numbers to indicate their answer)

- Independent writing where every student writes a response for a dedicated amount of time (for the youngest students, this may look like writing a word or drawing a picture in response to a prompt)

- Think-pair-share (students process a question or problem with a partner before moving on to whole-class discussion)

- Cold call (every student considers a question before they are called on by a teacher)

Many more techniques and variations are possible. These examples represent general categories of techniques teachers can deploy, though their effectiveness will depend on the quality of prior instruction and the clarity of the teacher's directions.

Teachers are often frustrated by students' low-quality answers, but such answers can often be traced back to inadequate preparation. A 3rd grader who does not know the kind of literary evidence they need to explain a character's traits will likely provide an inadequate response during their think-pair-share. Students who have yet to discuss patterns in number sequences will struggle when asked to complete a backward skip-counting pattern on their whiteboards. Remember, great critical thinking is grounded in the *knowledge* students are gaining. Students won't be able to do interesting tasks or explain their reasoning if they lack the knowledge to do so.

These techniques are ways of requiring every student to participate in the thinking work of the lesson, but they are also opportunities for the teacher to assess and determine the solidity of their class's understanding. (Chapter 5 will talk more about assessment and feedback.) Rather than posing easy opinion questions that don't actually assess depths of understanding, we can use questioning to ground students' thinking in the content they are learning.

What About Collaboration?

Some readers may wonder why there has not been a larger discussion of collaboration among students in this chapter. Often, critical thinking is associated with the ability to work in groups and to pursue projects.

The Critical Thinking Framework is agnostic in the battle over pedagogical styles. A wide range of classrooms and approaches will benefit from building explicit knowledge and structuring total participation techniques to ensure every student is included in the learning. For teachers and their coaches, the goal is to help every student learn and succeed in their classroom, no matter what stance their school, district, or curriculum takes on educational philosophy.

That said, some ways are more effective than others at structuring partnerships and small groups. Creating routines with partnerships and small groups that require every student to participate will help every student recall and practice the content they are learning. It will also make it easier to surface and address misunderstandings. Students can have easy-to-remember role

names, like the "peanut butter partner" and the "jelly partner." Some teachers may prefer simple A–D labels for group members. Labels like these will
help teachers efficiently assign roles and ask questions so no one in the group
dominates the thinking work.

Remember that students will need explicit criteria for what collaboration
can and should look like. Expectations for students to actively listen to one
another, take notes, or ask one another questions need to be clearly explained,
modeled, and practiced. Rolling out quality routines for partnerships and
small groups is a slow, labor-intensive process for the teacher, but if you want
your students to work effectively with one another, you have to take the same
approach with instruction as with any other important subject. Students
are not able to read chapter books at the beginning of reading instruction.
They first need to learn the foundational components in incremental chunks,
which will likely require months of sustained practice. In the same way, students may not start out knowing how to work productively in partnerships or
groups. The components of that complex skill need to be explicitly explained,
modeled, and practiced.

At the beginning of the year, I engage students in discussions about
appropriate norms for partner work. Depending on the age and group, we
either coconstruct the norms or I present criteria that the class can revise.
Typically, the norms include the following:

- Use kind, encouraging words.

- Partners work together at the same pace.

- Partners don't do the work for the other person. If one person is confused, the other partner can explain their thinking and steps out loud.
  Then the partner can try again.

- It's OK if partners don't agree! Depending on the disagreement, partners can

  ○ Look for ways to combine their ideas.

  ○ Try a different strategy to double-check their work. If they still
    can't agree, reach out to the teacher.

We go through a similar process with small-group work. When we first
engage in partner and small-group tasks, we pause frequently to check in on

how we're doing with our norms. Usually, students need a few weeks practicing the norms with low-stakes activities before they can perform more rigorous collaborative tasks.

All the pitfalls described at the beginning of this chapter can come into play during collaborative work. Some students may participate more than others; some may not deeply process the content; some may be overwhelmed by managing both the content and social demands. We need to supervise students closely to disrupt and address these pitfalls before and when they arise. As with teacher-led discussions, some teachers will avoid collaborative activities because of these potential pitfalls. The solution is the same, however: effective teacher planning can prepare the learning environment and the students for collaboration.

Conclusion

Teaching and learning make for a long road riddled with potholes. Through careful presentations of material, thoughtful questions, and total participation structures, teachers and students can navigate these pitfalls. Do not mistake me: this kind of planning is difficult. For teachers in resource-rich schools and districts with excellent curriculum materials, some of these tasks are already completed. The curriculum contains learning tasks that likely meet the criteria for students to engage in deep processing and rich discussions. Nevertheless, the materials should be reviewed to ensure that they suit students' needs. Teachers working in settings where these kinds of investments haven't been made and teachers who are trying to address areas of growth in their otherwise fine curriculum need to know how to fill in the gaps.

Chapter 4 Key Points

- Three common pitfalls can undermine student learning: shallow processing, overwhelmed working memory, and an overreliance on volunteers.

- Teachers can address these common pitfalls by chunking standards into smaller learning objectives, planning lesson activities that require students to make meaning, preparing questions for teacher-led discussions, and requiring all students to respond with total participation techniques.

- Teachers may also want to use collaborative structures, like partner and small-group work, as part of their instruction. Such structures are still vulnerable to the pitfalls, however, so planning to teach students how to collaborate should take them into account.

Further Reading

- *Why Don't Students Like School? A Cognitive Scientist Answers Questions About How the Mind Works and What It Means for the Classroom* by Daniel T. Willingham

- *How Learning Happens: Seminal Works in Educational Psychology and What They Mean in Practice* by Carl Hendrick and Paul Kirschner

5 CYCLES OF ASSESSMENT AND FEEDBACK

Every six to eight weeks, most elementary schools use some assessment system to evaluate reading. During one such period, I was giving students individual assessments that included a running record (where students read a passage aloud) and comprehension questions. Even though teachers are supposed to postpone their judgments about students until after an assessment, I, like most of my peers, had made a number of predictions based on my classroom experiences. I had two students, Lana and Peter, who were about to take the same reading assessment. I figured that Lana would fail and Peter would pass. Both Lana and Peter would be able to decode the passage, sure, but Lana tended to be quieter in group discussions, and Peter was quicker with an idea. I assumed Lana's reticence was because she struggled to make inferences about characters, whereas Peter often had many potential theories. When we sat down for the assessment, Lana and Peter both read the passage fluently and with expression; however, things took a turn on the comprehension questions. It turned out that Peter had no clue about the plot of the story, which led to a number of nonsensical ideas about the characters. Lana, however, understood the factual events of the story and easily responded to questions about the character's motivations.

Before proceeding, I should note that I have become increasingly skeptical about the effectiveness of leveled reading assessments, especially in light of what we know about the importance of background knowledge and vocabulary in reading comprehension. Perhaps that factor played a part in why Lana understood the story and Peter didn't. Either way, the situation illustrates why assessments are a crucial part of teaching and learning, even assessments in need of improvement. Based on my subjective experiences with the students, I thought I could predict who would be successful and who would not. I was correct in my prediction about decoding, but I was far off on how well the students would comprehend the events and characters in the story. Teachers are often skilled at observing and diagnosing misunderstandings in students, but our subjective observations are not sufficiently thorough. We inevitably miss things. Assessments help us check our individual biases by providing an impersonal representation of student ability.

You might be thinking, "Wait a second. Why are we talking about assessments right now? This is a book about critical thinking! Aren't the goals of assessment and critical thinking naturally opposed? Aren't tests just another way to narrow the curriculum and prevent students from learning a wide breadth of subjects and content? The goal should be to reduce or even eliminate assessments in school."

My short answer is no.

The rest of the chapter is my long answer.

Who's Afraid of the Big Bad Test?

There are a lot of bad tests out there. As a teacher and a student, I have been on both sides of some awful tests. Tests that didn't seem to know which standards they were assessing. Tests with poorly designed questions. Tests given in horrendous, nonstandardized settings. Tests that were redundant and a waste of everyone's time. Tests that, if they were widespread practice, would justify doing away with the entire concept of testing.

Not all tests need to be that way.

As I mentioned, teachers are not neutral arbiters of their students' progress. We know a lot, and our on-the-ground knowledge of our classes should carry significant weight in any discussion of a student's academic achievement. Nevertheless, in the same way a test cannot paint a complete picture of a student, neither can the observations of one teacher. Tests or assessments help develop a more holistic picture of students' academic performance by making visible their otherwise invisible thinking. As a result, assessments *help* teachers support students in developing and refining their thinking processes.

In fact, we have already started talking about the role of assessments in teaching and learning. Chapter 4 discussed total participation techniques, such as using whiteboards or gestures, which act as a type of assessment. This chapter focuses on two types of assessments:

- **Formative assessments** are informal assessments teachers give throughout a lesson, or even at the end of a lesson, to check for student understanding of the content taught. Formative assessment typically assesses one specific learning goal.

- **Summative assessments** are formal assessments given at the end of a learning sequence, such as a unit or term. Summative assessments can be reading benchmarks, unit tests, one-on-one student interviews and inventories, and more. Summative assessments typically assess multiple learning goals.

Both formative and summative assessments allow teachers to evaluate the breadth and depth of student content knowledge, and all types of assessments help teachers ascertain students' understanding and provide thoughtful academic feedback. We can use the Critical Thinking Framework to support giving quality feedback to students.

Despite their bad reputation, tests do have merit for learners. Frequent low-stakes tests can lead to higher long-term memory gains for individuals. The phenomenon is often called "the testing effect"—when students take tests requiring them to retrieve previously learned information from long-term memory, even when they have difficulty recalling a particular idea or concept, the act of retrieval reinforces the information in long-term memory (Endres & Renkl, 2015). When individuals have an opportunity to see what they do not know, especially when they receive feedback or see their errors corrected, they are better equipped to revise their misunderstandings or focus their attention on filling in knowledge gaps when studying (Roediger et al., 2011). Frequent quizzes that ask students to recall information are more effective at improving recall than no tests or restudying.

What does this mean for our youngest students? To achieve our ambitious vision for students, we can harness the best practices of testing and assessment for their benefit. Luckily, most early grades employ a number of these best practices already, especially when students are learning to read. Students are first introduced to a sound or phonics rule, and then have to recall the rule through frequent reading and spelling practice. Teachers or peers can offer quick feedback during this practice. Unfortunately, elementary classrooms do not always deploy these same effective practices in other subjects. Frequent low-stakes quizzes in vocabulary, math facts, skip-counting, and other types of factual knowledge can strengthen student recall when asked to solve complex problems. Hardly the enemy, informal tests can in fact help students lacking in certain prerequisite knowledge practice the skills they need to do rigorous, grade-level work. Quizzes are as much a learning technique as they are a tool for assessment. They can be a tool to solidify concepts in long-term memory, including concepts that were once novel and complex for students. As new concepts are fluently recalled and applied, students develop proficiency with problems and tasks of greater complexity and rigor.

Putting the politics of high-stakes state tests aside, we have a number of good reasons to use assessments consistently in our classrooms. As both a learning tool and a magnifying glass, properly planned and executed assessments can help students and teachers engage in productive learning sequences. But assessments should not be used for evaluation alone—the purpose of assessment should be to hone and improve learning. The purpose of assessment should be to support *feedback.*

Assessment for Feedback

We cannot talk about assessment without talking about feedback. If we want to provide our students with targeted, helpful feedback, we need to use a range of assessments to surface and address misunderstandings. Assessment and feedback are intertwined—neither is effective or purposeful without the other.

What do we mean by feedback? Similar to critical thinking, the word *feedback* has been thrown around in a number of contexts. Teachers are told repeatedly to provide "high-quality" feedback to students, leaving the definition implicit in the advice. In the research literature about feedback, one of the most influential definitions comes from Arkalgud Ramaprasad (1983): "Feedback is information about the gap between the actual level and the reference level of a system parameter which is used to alter the gap in some way" (p. 4). This definition is technical, but useful when translated into plain terms: feedback is information that closes the gap between actual performance and desired performance. For teachers, this looks like knowing the expected outcomes for student performance and knowing where your students actually are now. Assessment *reveals* student performance. Feedback should then *improve* student performance so they progress toward the goals of their subject and grade.

But not all feedback is effective (Kluger & DeNisi, 1996), nor is feedback the exclusive domain of teachers. The goal of feedback is not just for students to depend on their teachers to evaluate their work, but for students eventually to provide themselves with feedback or even judge the quality of feedback they are receiving from others. For novice learners, self-assessment is unlikely to be effective in the early stages of learning a new content area. Nevertheless, consistent and credible feedback can lay the groundwork to transition students to a place where they can provide themselves and others with feedback. As students move along the novice–expert spectrum, they can depend less on their teacher and more on themselves and their peers.

Teachers want to serve the needs of individual students with targeted feedback, but those needs will differ significantly from learner to learner in a heterogeneous classroom. What are the best ways to go about targeting feedback? Sometimes we are advised to meet in long, individual conferences with each student to suss out their particular strengths and weaknesses. The actual substance of these conversations might range from explorative questioning to providing a crisp "glow" and "grow" for the student. Other times we are told to create elaborate tracking systems and checklists to monitor students during independent work times. There is a lot of gold to mine in these suggestions. But a one-size-fits-all vision of feedback can leave teachers too rigid to respond effectively to what they are seeing in student work. Rather than give teachers a "recipe" for feedback, I outline a thinking process teachers can use to help them make decisions about when and how to give feedback.

The process begins with high-level planning. School teams can start to realize their ambitious visions by designing a summative assessment plan and evaluating the curriculum pacing calendar. The ambitious vision, assessment plan, and pacing calendar become a "master plan," which will anchor teacher planning and execution throughout the year.

Create a Summative Assessment Plan and Pacing Calendar

We've discussed some important reasons why assessment and feedback matter in our classrooms. But for teachers and administrators, the first question is, where do we start? The answer is, before kids enter the building. A clear plan for summative assessments throughout the year should be in place before the school year begins. Look at the curriculum, along with your ambitious vision for student achievement, and think about where to schedule unit assessments and interim assessments to monitor student progress. Think of these assessments as checkpoints to see whether kids are truly learning—and *retaining*—what they have been taught.

For schools and classrooms prioritizing ambitious goals for their students, it is important to begin the year with a clear accounting of where students are in their academic achievement. In elementary school classrooms, teachers can use a number of low-lift diagnostic assessments to evaluate their students at the beginning of the school year:

- With individual students, read decodable passages to assess accuracy and fluency.

- Use a spelling inventory to see what spelling rules students know and don't know.

- Post a writing prompt and have students write for 15–30 minutes (depending on their age). Compare this on-demand writing to the writing samples from your ambitions vision.

- Assign students a handful of math problems from the previous grade to assess retention and mastery.

- Make a list of prerequisite skills students need to be successful in the current grade's math standards. Assess students on just these prerequisite skills to see if they need any proactive instruction.

As mentioned, assessments must be considered in concert with feedback. While creating a summative assessment overview for the year, planners need to keep an eye on the curriculum pacing calendar. Sometimes referred to as a scope and sequence, the pacing calendar outlines when lessons and learning standards will be taught over the course of a school year. Typically, the pacing calendar is simply seen as a compliance tool—it helps ensure the curriculum is covered in a specified period of time. Teachers have no excuse but to finish teaching all of the curriculum material by June.

But compliance alone does not fully realize the potential of this planning process. The pacing calendar can be so much more than that! A pacing calendar is about ensuring not just coverage of learning goals but actual learning. Before a single class bell rings, the pacing calendar can structure opportunities for teachers to execute meaningful, assessment-based feedback.

Planners should look at their calendar and ask these questions:

- Following a summative assessment, is there space in the pacing calendar for teachers to respond to student needs? How and when can we build in days for teachers to respond to trends they see on assessments?

- Is there space in the pacing calendar to respond to trends arising from formative assessments? Are teachers forced to move on to new learning objectives, or are they given flexible days where they can extend or shorten a learning sequence in response to student needs?

Flexibility must be built into pacing calendars for teachers to respond effectively to their students. While planners may anticipate some situations, every class of students will react to new content slightly differently than another class. Teachers who are in a new grade or have a class with varying levels of skills may need flexibility to plan and execute high-quality responses to their class's needs.

Here's the rub: although some teachers and grade-level teams can make big-picture decisions around summative assessments, these decisions are often made by school administrators. Teachers who are currently not part of schoolwide discussions about assessment and pacing must not be afraid to give concrete feedback to the people who are. The more specificity shared with the people engaged in this high-level planning, the more effective the calendars. And for readers who happen to be administrators, it is critical to include teachers in pacing calendar discussions. They know where they need flexibility, and they can let you know which units will require additional days. They may even just need a bank of days they can use as needed throughout the year. The point is to talk to teachers about what they need to be truly responsive to their students. Pacing calendars can systematize sustainable planning and responsive teaching, and they should not be shuffled to the back of a forgotten binder or used as an accountability cudgel.

In my own experience, I like to use flex days differently based on the subject. For math, I prefer to distribute flex days throughout units. These pause points allow me either to address a trend I'm noticing within the unit I'm teaching or to incorporate targeted review of material learned earlier in the year. For ELA, I use flex days to buffer writing projects, which students sometimes need more time with to produce high-quality work. I also use ELA flex days to supplement the curriculum with read-alouds that reflect the diversity of my class while reinforcing unit learning standards. Figure 5.1 depicts a pacing calendar with flex days both distributed weekly and added to allow for post-assessment instruction.

Clear Goals and Outcomes

Even once a summative assessment plan and pacing calendar are created, the work is not done. For assessments to be tools for feedback, the assessments themselves need to be aligned to clear goals and outcomes. This is the time to create or revisit the ambitious vision you have for your students. What do you want to see in the student work? What is an end-of-year exemplar versus an exemplar from different checkpoints throughout the year?

These checkpoints help teachers plan for formative assessment techniques. Because teachers primarily implement formative assessment during daily lessons and summative assessments less frequently, specific benchmarks and checkpoints throughout the year will help them know what kind of student work they are looking for. Teachers can use the checklist process outlined in Chapter 3 to annotate exemplars of student work and codify criteria they are looking for in their lessons.

FIGURE 5.1

Pacing Calendar Excerpt

In this sample pacing calendar, flex days are distributed so that teachers can do a reteach or review lesson every Wednesday (U = unit, L = lesson). When possible, flex days are added after a test to allow time to address any trends seen on the test.

	Kindergarten	1st Grade	2nd Grade	3rd Grade	4th Grade	5th Grade
10/3	U1, L12	U1, L15	U1, L8	U1, L10	U2, L2	U1, L9
10/4	U1, L13	Test	U1, L9	U1, L11	U2, L3	U1, L10
10/5	Flex	Flex	Flex	Flex	Flex	Flex
10/6	U1, L14	U2, L1	U1, L10	U1, L12	U2, L4	U1, L11
10/7	U1, L15	U2, L2	U1, L11	U1, L13	U2, L5	U1, L12
10/10	Holiday					
10/11	U1, L16	U2, L3	U1, L12	U1, L14	U2, L6	U1, L13
10/12	Flex	Flex	Flex	Flex	Flex	Flex
10/13	Test	U2, L4	U1, L13	U1, L15	U2, L7	U1, L14
10/14	Flex	U2, L5	U1, L14	Test	U2, L8	U1, L15

It's important to remember that exemplars represent *independent* student performance, not student performance based on feedback. As mentioned earlier, novice learners need feedback and are not prepared to effectively self-assess right away. However, as novice learners receive consistent feedback and become more independent with the skills they learned, they become more capable of assessing themselves and others. This level of independence is impossible without clear goals and outcomes. Teachers should look at the checklists they created (refer back to Chapter 3) to help them determine what students can and cannot do independently right now. They can then use responsive feedback to fill in these gaps and move students toward independence. Chapter 6 offers specific examples of ways for teachers to implement responsive feedback.

A Note to Leaders

After assembling a bird's-eye view of assessment, curriculum pacing, and an ambitious vision of student achievement, the real work begins. The goal is to create a virtuous cycle of assessment and feedback that propels student understanding forward.

District, school, and grade-level leaders should keep some questions in mind regarding this assessment and feedback cycle in which teachers need to thoughtfully respond to what they are seeing in the classroom. Consider the instructional blocks currently in your school's schedule: do they actually allow teachers to address feedback to the whole group, to small groups, and to individuals? If not, how can you adjust your instructional blocks to build in that kind of flexibility? Do teacher observation and evaluation mechanisms leave time and space for teachers to make strategic decisions in response to student work? Are teachers afraid to be seen supporting struggling students? Or are teachers only praised when no student is seen to struggle with the material?

A virtuous cycle of assessment and feedback is only possible when teachers are able to make decisions both in the moment and during their planning process. Teachers need supportive professional environments where they can focus on the challenging work in front of them. This work is not surface-level work—it is intellectually challenging, and teachers need the time to do it. In the same way a pacing calendar can support or inhibit effective instruction, so can decisions around instructional design, scheduling, and coaching. If you're a leader who is excited about leveraging the power of assessment and feedback to improve student thinking, begin by thinking about how the larger structures in your school can act as either barriers or bridges to better outcomes.

A Virtuous Cycle

We've established which big-picture structures need to be in place at the very beginning of the year—a summative assessment plan, a pacing calendar, and an ambitious vision for student work. These structures will produce the conditions for teachers to practice cycles of assessment and feedback on a daily and monthly basis.

Even though a summative assessment schedule will identify helpful check-in points to see where students are compared to their annual learning goals, the most important cycle of assessment and feedback occurs within and around daily instruction. Formative assessments paired with quick, targeted feedback embedded in daily lessons generate a cycle of learning and improvement for students. This cycle is a mental model teachers can use in their lesson planning and execution (see Figure 5.2).

FIGURE 5.2

Virtuous Cycle of Instruction, Assessment, and Feedback

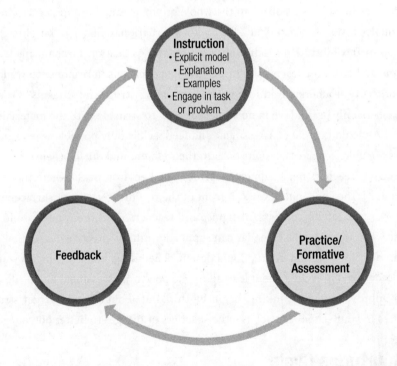

There are a number of ways to structure a lesson. We can stick to the I-We-You model, or we may use an inquiry model where students first engage in an exploratory activity before receiving any direct instruction. These and many other variations are more effective when combined with cycles of formative assessment and feedback. In most lessons, teachers open with a model of a learning objective, an explanation, examples of content, or a task or problem. They may even use a combination of these approaches. After the initial learning and engagement, the teacher provides opportunities for practice. This is where formative assessment can come in, which typically looks like asking students a question or assigning a task.

Chapter 4 discussed the concept that not every question and task are created equal. When planning for formative assessment, avoid participation techniques that reduce the number of students engaged in thinking during the lesson. If we care about giving every student in our classroom quality feedback to improve their thinking, then every student needs to be thinking. Avoid self-assessment questions about confidence or understanding. Unless the stakes of a moment are low, use total participation techniques rather than relying on volunteers.

As students practice, look for trends. What do they understand? What do they not understand? Are there specific misconceptions bubbling to the surface that you anticipated? (Refer back to the What/How/Oops chart in Figure 3.3.) This is where you have an opportunity to provide feedback, though whether the feedback is targeted to an individual, small group, or whole group will depend on the trends you see. After receiving feedback, students should practice again. Once again, formative assessment can reveal how students responded to the feedback. At this point, you may decide to continue the feedback–formative assessment cycle, or you may see that students are ready to receive additional instruction. Chapter 6 further explores the thinking process for feedback.

Some teachers may have the flexibility and capacity to lead students through 5–10 cycles in a single block, while others may only complete 1 or 2. The number of feedback cycles also depends on the content being taught. We want to maximize the quality feedback students receive, but we aren't always able to give them a high quantity of feedback. More important than the number of cycles in a given day is the consistency of the assessment–feedback cycle. These cycles are most effective when they are a routine part of a teacher's planning and lesson execution.

The cycle of assessment and feedback can only be virtuous as long as it is sustained. With opportunities to practice and receive feedback, students progress toward their learning goals. In between lessons, teachers can use student work from previous lessons to adjust their instruction and make their feedback even more purposeful (see Figure 5.3). Based on what we know about working and long-term memory, mastery of learning goals—especially ambitious ones—simply cannot be done in a single day or even in a few days. Practice must take place over a prolonged period—sometimes over the course of weeks, months, or even years—to truly be rooted in long-term memory.

FIGURE 5.3

Effects of Regular Assessment–Feedback Cycles

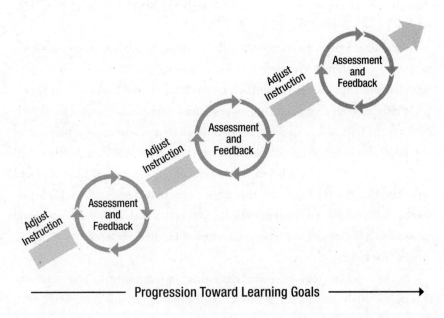

Teachers, don't despair! While elementary school teachers usually only have their students for one year, the learning goals for students in primary grades are the building blocks for high-level reading, writing, and math. With rich practice and feedback, you are helping students establish a strong foundation that will serve them for years to come.

When the Cycle Turns Vicious

The goal of feedback cycles within a lesson and across a series of lessons is to close the gap between students' current performance and desired performance. As students receive feedback and refine their thinking about learned content, they grow in both competence and confidence.

But feedback isn't always beneficial. Sometimes feedback can have negative effects, causing performance to worsen rather than improve (Kluger & DeNisi, 1996). Consistently ineffective feedback produces a vicious, rather than virtuous, cycle of learning.

How do we tell the difference between effective and ineffective forms of feedback? Chapter 6 presents short- and long-term responses to improve student performance. Until that point, here are some important principles to remember:

- Clear criteria must be used to assess performance. If we do not know what we are looking for, we won't be able to explain it to students. Your checklist of excellent student work from Chapter 3 can help guide this work.

- Students need an opportunity to use feedback. If students do not have an opportunity to practice and implement the feedback we give them, it will make very little difference. In elementary school, especially, we can expect students to need multiple opportunities to practice before they can become independent with a learning objective.

- Feedback needs to make sense. Sometimes we lecture a student about what we want to see, but the explanation itself provides no guidance. We need to use concise, transparent language to communicate feedback.

- Feedback should encourage a positive mindset about learning. Feedback that implies students are incapable of doing a task will likely discourage them from implementing helpful changes. Feedback does not need to coddle students or mislead them about their performance, but we should use it to motivate students toward improvement. Students with depleted self-esteem are unlikely to keep practicing or believe they will get better. They are more likely to give up.

One of the best ways to tell whether feedback is effective is to look at assessments. Summative assessment checkpoints and in-class formative assessments will tell us whether our interventions are working. If students are not improving or are doing worse following teacher feedback, then we need to step back and adjust our instruction. We also need to remain attentive to our students; their body language and verbal reactions will help us see the immediate impact of our feedback. In the last chapter, we will discuss how to help our students see challenge and error as an exciting part of the learning process.

Conclusion

In the opening of this chapter, I shared the story of how my own judgments about students were incorrect. I would not have known my error without an external assessment. Without the assessment, I would have given both students unhelpful feedback, which would not have improved their reading performance at all. Not only do assessments help teachers uncover and investigate their own biases, they can also reveal ways to improve instruction.

Schools aiming to improve the quality of student thinking will benefit from using cycles of assessment and feedback. No matter how hard we try, we cannot see inside the heads of students. Summative and formative assessments help demystify some of the thinking processes our students use, knowledge that we can then leverage to close the gap between present and desired student performance.

Some of this sounds a little mechanical: teachers pursue a certain set of inputs, and students produce desired outputs. It's important to remember the assessment–feedback cycle is a model to help teachers think about their instruction, but the effectiveness of the model depends on the nitty-gritty judgments they make. Teachers and students are constantly responding to one another, and teacher's contributions cannot be easily reduced into simple inputs and outputs. Chapter 6 explores both short- and long-term feedback.

Chapter 5 Key Points

- Tests are both an assessment and a learning tool.

- Summative and formative assessments provide teachers with the information they need to give students feedback.

- Feedback should close the gap between students' current and desired performance.

- Assessment plans and pacing calendars can work in concert to help teachers track student achievement and respond to student needs.

- Cycles of formative assessment and feedback should occur in every lesson. When assessment and feedback are sustained over the course of the year, they create a virtuous cycle that supports student growth.

- Ineffective feedback over time can create a vicious cycle, which undermines student learning and achievement. Teachers should monitor the quality of their feedback to ensure it makes a positive impact on their students.

FEEDBACK:
A THOUGHT PROCESS

Chapter 5 focused on creating the overarching structures of a summative assessment plan, pacing calendar, and daily formative assessment–feedback cycle, to propel student learning. Now we turn to the decisions teachers make during assessment–feedback cycles to address student knowledge and skill gaps. We will explore a method teachers and instructional coaches can use to think through their responses to formative and summative assessments. Once assessments reveal understanding and misunderstanding, teachers need to use their judgment to come up with feedback that will improve student performance. This approach is part of a larger thinking process teachers can use to make a wide range of instructional decisions around feedback and academic interventions.

When considering feedback, I use the following process:

- Prepare for feedback.
- Determine who needs feedback and for what.
- Choose an appropriate short-term or long-term response.

First, let's look at how teachers can prepare for feedback before a lesson or unit, which helps them determine *who* needs feedback and for *what*. Then we'll consider recommendations for feedback in three different settings: whole group, small group, and individual. In each setting, once they have identified the learning gap, teachers can decide whether they need to pursue a short-term or long-term response. A short-term response may occur in the moment or within a day or two. A long-term response will require larger adjustments to instruction across multiple days or weeks.

You may notice that some of the short-term and long-term responses can be used at other times or in other settings. I want to emphasize that this section focuses on a *thinking process*. I offer recommendations for cutoffs and possible feedback interventions, but teachers should use their judgment about when and how to apply them. As a teacher, I have endured endless frustration when dealing with rigid rubrics that, if allowed to wholly supplant my own judgment, would lead to less effective and less efficient practices. I don't want to mislead you—so much of my personal learning and growth has come from interactions with well-prepared instructional materials, whether rubrics, frameworks, or fundamentals of instruction. Such tools helped me build necessary background knowledge and hone my internal thinking processes so I can make better and better decisions in my classroom. In a similar way, my goal is to present flexible principles that can be incorporated into a thoughtful practitioner's repertoire.

Prepare for Feedback

When assessing students, we are looking for which thinking processes and academic habits are evident in their work and which require more support. We should take students and their current thought patterns seriously, especially since most kids are trying their best to make sense of the content in front of them. We ask, "What was the student thinking when they did _____?" The answer helps us determine whether students are missing crucial content knowledge or whether they are struggling to employ elements of the Critical Thinking Framework to make sense of what they are learning.

The process outlined in Chapter 3 is useful when preparing to give students feedback. Before beginning a new unit or a lesson, create or review a checklist of what student work should include, as well as what prerequisite skills students will require to be successful in producing exemplary student work. Make and reflect on a What/How/Oops chart to anticipate where students will struggle.

The Critical Thinking Framework can help teaching teams think through the What/How/Oops charts and checklists. As described in the case studies in Chapter 2, teachers can use the framework as prompts. How would a student say _____ in their own words? What structures and underlying principles should students see across the unit? How will a student express questions or misconceptions? As a reminder, here are the Critical Thinking Framework components:

- **Say it in your own words.** Students articulate ideas in their own words. They use unique phrasing and do not parrot the explanations of others.

- **Break it down.** Students break down the components, steps, or smaller ideas within a bigger idea or procedure.

- **Look for structure.** Students look beyond shallow surface characteristics to see deep structures and underlying principles.

- **Notice gaps and inconsistencies in ideas.** Students ask questions about gaps and inconsistencies in material, arguments, and their own thinking.

- **Reason with evidence.** Students construct arguments with evidence and evaluate the evidence in others' reasoning.

These components help teachers and grade-level teams think about their students' thinking. How are students successful in their thinking process? How are they struggling? By breaking down objectives according to the Critical Thinking Framework, we can efficiently diagnose where students are successful and where they need to improve in their thinking.

When preparing to provide feedback, you must give each subject its due. In other words, try not to project performance in one subject onto another. Remember, a student may be able to beautifully summarize the main ideas in a nonfiction text about bird adaptations but struggle to explain the concept of an equivalent fraction. Students need to develop their expertise in every subject, and we should not assume success in one domain will predict success in another, even when that domain may seem similar on the surface.

While this preparation may feel tedious at first, it will help you make faster and more strategic decisions when responding to students. A common expression resonates here: you have to go slow to go fast. Going slow in your preparation enables you to move faster in your responses to students later. Your time, and your students' time, will be more productive. No matter how much you may want to, don't skimp during this step.

Determine Who Needs Feedback and for What

How do we figure out who needs feedback? And what do they need feedback for? After the beginning of the year diagnostic assessment, we may already know who will need feedback and additional support for a set of objectives. These assessments may reveal gaps in prerequisite knowledge, which we can proactively address in whole-group, small-group, and individual settings. If we haven't given a diagnostic assessment or simply didn't capture student competency in an area, we will need to answer these questions during the formative assessment cycle or following summative assessment checkpoints.

There are a few ways to capture who needs feedback and for what. One common practice is to create a tracker on a clipboard and use it to monitor students by writing student names in one column and checking off which learning components they are demonstrating. Figure 6.1 is an example of a tracker used for a 1st grade math lesson on fractions. A check mark (✓) indicates the student is successfully accomplishing the objective, while a delta symbol (Δ) means the student is unable to do the skill or needs support to meet the objective.

During student practice, a teacher who is checking off whether students are meeting the learning objectives of the lesson very quickly notices if one, some, or a majority of the students are confused. If most students can partition a shape through the center and correctly label the parts of a fraction, but they can't explain that ¼ is smaller than ½, the teacher knows what the entire class misunderstands. If all but one or two students demonstrate understanding of the learning objectives, then the teacher can direct attention to giving feedback to those one or two students. If the students are unable to meet any of the objectives across the board, the teacher knows either there was an issue with their initial instruction or they are missing critical prerequisites to access the content of the lesson.

FIGURE 6.1

Tracker for 1st Grade Fractions Lesson

Student	Partitioned shape through center	Correctly labeled parts (½ or ¼)	Could explain that ¼ is less than ½
Aisha M.	✓	✓	✓
Eric P.	✓	✓	✓
Mirabel E.	✓	✓	Δ
Bruno L.	✓	Δ	Δ
Anna F.	✓	✓	Δ
Ella Q.	✓	Δ	Δ
Henry P.	✓	✓	Δ
Talib O.	✓	✓	✓

✓ = Student is successfully accomplishing objective.
Δ = Student is unable to do skill or needs support in meeting objective.

Some teachers may prefer a more concise tracker where they capture notes about which students are struggling, rather than pausing to check off every student. Figure 6.2 shows the same lesson objectives as Figure 6.1, but in this one, the teacher jots down the initials of the students struggling with the objective. In this example, although the majority of students are successful at the first and third objectives, they are not correctly labeling the parts of the fraction. Depending on the number of students in the class, the number of names jotted down will trigger a whole-class, small-group, or individual response.

I need to pause here to make a confession: the trackers in Figure 6.1 and 6.2 are powerful tools to quickly determine who needs feedback and for what. I have used them, and I have trained others in how to create and use them. Nevertheless, these trackers are not always part of my daily lessons—at least not anymore. Instead, I cheat. I don't actually cheat, in the sense that I pretend like I'm monitoring students only to daydream as I sip my coffee. Instead, I use a shortcut: I count. Once I have internalized the two to three criteria I am looking for in high-quality student work, I circulate during student practice and count how many students need feedback on the different criteria. This is most similar to the tracker in Figure 6.2. In 10 years of classroom teaching, my class sizes have always been around 28–30 students. If three or fewer students need feedback on a key point or skill, I don't need to give the entire class that feedback—I can direct it to just those students. If I count five or more, I know the most efficient method is to give feedback either to a small group of students or to the whole group. Sometimes, if I have counted five students who need feedback but haven't finished circulating to every student, I pause the class to give feedback to the whole group. In my experience, if you encounter five or more students confused before you even get halfway around the room, you'll probably find at least four to five more students by the end of your circuit.

FIGURE 6.2

Alternate Tracker for 1st Grade Fractions Lesson

Partitioned shape through center	Correctly labeled parts (½ or ¼)	Could explain that ¼ is less than ½
AM BL	EP AF AM BL LP TO ME	ME

Teachers new to monitoring student work for trends in understanding and misunderstanding should not begin by counting. For one, it takes time to know whether you are seeing students successfully meet your expectations, and teachers who are learning to evaluate student practice should go slowly at first. You may not get through as many assessment and feedback cycles, but that's OK. It's better to do fewer cycles and offer students more thoughtful feedback than to go slow and misdiagnose what students need. I recommend starting with one of the trackers in Figures 6.1 and 6.2. As you become more fluent at observing students in their practice, you may devise a shortcut of your own to speed up the monitoring process.

Once teachers have a system to monitor formative assessments, they can use the data gathered during student practice to make a decision. Monitoring student practice will tell teachers *who* needs feedback and for *what*, but it will not tell teachers *how* and *when* to deliver feedback. They need to consider a number of important questions. For example, is this the kind of feedback that can be given in the moment, or is this the kind of feedback that needs to change the substance of lessons moving forward? Is this a quick fix or a deeper misconception?

Once you have determined, through either summative or formative assessments, who needs feedback, you have a number of options. The following sections go through the thinking process for whole-group, small-group, and individual feedback, with both short-term and long-term responses. You will notice that I give suggested cutoffs to trigger these types of feedback. These percentages and numbers are based on my experience teaching large class sizes, with an average of around 28 to 30. You may want to retool the cutoffs based on your own classroom.

Whole-Group Feedback

When to use: 10 or more students (approximately 30 percent) in a class share an error or misunderstanding.

Rationale: When eight or more students struggle with an error or misunderstanding, teachers should not let those errors fester, because students may end up practicing and reinforcing misconceptions. In the same way that teachers can help students build schemata in long-term memory to support their understanding, students can build erroneous schemata and mental models. When a significant number of students share the same misconception, it is not worth it for teachers to alter their class model by breaking students into groups (unless students are already purposefully grouped in the instructional block). It is much more efficient to address the whole group, which also allows the teacher to use the students who do understand to help demonstrate and explain concepts to others.

Whole-class feedback will look a little different based on whether the errors are due to missing prerequisite knowledge or only due to struggles with grade-level content. Feedback and interventions for missing prerequisite knowledge can often be integrated into different parts of the daily schedule. When a class requires feedback on grade-level content, the Critical Thinking Framework will help guide our feedback during the virtuous cycle of assessment and feedback.

Missing Prerequisite Knowledge

In the post-COVID-19 world, students in the United States are showing evidence of more learning gaps than ever before. Even before the pandemic and school closures, heterogeneous classrooms included students with varying levels of preparation. Teachers need short- and long-term ways to address gaps to make grade-level instruction accessible to all students.

I want to acknowledge how challenging this work is. In a perfect world, teachers would not need to be concerned with integrating the learning goals of previous grades. In that world, ambitious visions and high expectations would be the norm, and remediation would be reserved for special circumstances. Unfortunately, the United States has neither national standards nor a national curriculum, and expectations of and results from students can vary greatly by state, region, city, neighborhood, school, and even classroom. Teachers and schools, however, must not surrender in the face of these challenges. In elementary schools especially, we can mitigate the effects of missed learning before they snowball into years of lost instruction. Elementary schools are best situated to give students a sturdy foundation before they move on to more advanced grades and subjects. Our short-term and long-term responses to missing prerequisite knowledge can reorient a student's academic trajectory.

Short-Term Responses

Most instances of lacking prerequisite knowledge will require a long-term response to shore up the skills of the entire class. Nevertheless, sometimes teachers can respond to a class need in the moment or the next day, such as when the prerequisite is something students can learn and master very quickly (e.g., vocabulary definitions or pronunciations).

- **Share information with students either at the beginning of the lesson or in the moment.** Post a definition or share a visual to quickly clarify the meaning. *"Class, today we are going to see the word* sum *in* *our math work. A* sum *is the answer, or total, when we add numbers together. If you see 'Find the sum' or 'What is the sum?' it means you are adding numbers."*

- **Present students with a model.** Most short-term responses to fill in a knowledge gap need only take a few minutes, and sometimes as little as 30 seconds. *"When we read three-digit numbers, I hear students saying, 'One hundred and twenty-three.' It's actually 'One hundred twenty-three.' Let's read a few together. My turn, your turn."*

Long-Term Responses

Long-term responses to address knowledge gaps usually require some alteration to instructional blocks and additional planning. Teachers don't need to do away with the grade-level curriculum in order to reteach the previous grade, but instead should incorporate practice with prerequisite skills into daily instruction. These are the essential skills students need to know to accomplish the learning objectives successfully. For instance, students need to be able to skip-count to access multiplication and division, know how to write a complete sentence before they can write a paragraph, and track the plot of a fiction text before they can infer the main character's motivations.

For long-term responses to be successful, school teams cannot skip the *preparation for feedback* step. To determine the prerequisite knowledge required to meet a learning objective or fulfill an ambitious vision, teachers and instructional leaders need to sit down and analyze their grade-level standards and student work exemplars, and then generate a list of knowledge and skills students will need. Assessment will also play an important role in this process. Diagnostic assessments, or summative assessments from the end of the previous year, will give valuable insights into what prerequisite knowledge students still need to acquire.

While some long-term responses require only 5–10 minutes of daily interventions, others require teachers to significantly modify their instructional blocks and lesson plans. The suggestions laid out here move along a "low-lift" to "high-lift" spectrum. The low-lift suggestions are ones teachers can implement with little planning and preparation. For the suggestions nearer the high-lift end of the spectrum, teachers and grade-level teams will need to do more work to alter their instruction to accommodate the needs of students.

- **Establish daily academic routines to reinforce important factual knowledge.** Teachers can lead students in these routines, which should last no more than five minutes, during transition periods, morning meetings, or calendar math, or they can reserve five minutes of an instructional block. Examples include skip-counting songs, math fact quizzes, a pop quiz where students quickly respond to questions on a whiteboard, a task to edit the morning message for conventions and mechanics errors, Make It Complete (students convert a sentence fragment into a complete sentence), and Magic Number (students determine a mystery number by listening to "greater than _____" and "less than _____" clues).

- **At the beginning of an instructional block, tell students they will engage in explicit practice around a prerequisite skill.** Teachers can call this period "fluency warmup," "do now," or "bell work." This practice should be short and focused on only one skill. For example, tell students exactly what you are working on with them. *"I'm noticing you have been struggling with this problem in math because we need some more practice with single-digit subtraction. We're going to do some quick practice at the beginning of the next few classes. I'm also going to give a couple of quizzes this week and next week to check in."*

- **Provide students with a supportive scaffold to be used in class, such as sentence starters or a visual anchor, to help them access the prerequisite skills they need to complete a more complex task.** When providing an entire class with a scaffold, remember to teach students *how* to use it. Any tool offered to students should be introduced with a clear model and explanation; otherwise, they may use the scaffold incorrectly or, worse, become more confused. Examples include sentence starters, word banks, number charts, visual anchors, graphic organizers, and text with important sections already highlighted.

- **Add flexible days to the beginning of a new unit to explicitly teach missing prerequisites.** Addressing prerequisites may take from less than one day to a few days to adequately teach, but don't postpone grade-level instruction for too long. The purpose of these flexible lessons is to prepare students to do grade-level work, not to replace grade-level work. For example, in a unit about calculating elapsed time, 3rd graders must first know the parts of the clock, how to skip-count by 5s and 10s, and how to set up a number line. In an ELA unit about historical fiction, 4th graders must first know different kinds of genres, such as fiction and nonfiction, as well as their characteristics.

• **Start the year with a "Unit 0."** Design an introductory unit where students spend the first two to four weeks of the year reviewing critical learning objectives from the past year. Each instructional block can be dedicated to shoring up prerequisite skills integral to grade-level instruction.

For emerging multilingual learners and students with exceptionalities, these types of daily interventions often align with their specific learning goals. Teachers should cross-check their plans with the goals and accommodations identified in students' individualized education plans (IEPs)—some activities may need to be adjusted to align with their mandated needs. For example, second grade students are reviewing complete sentences. Michael, a multilingual learner who also has a print-based learning disability, has a goal of writing a complete sentence with a subject and a predicate. In addition to engaging in the practice activities with his classmates, Michael needs a checklist with visuals and a teacher check-in before he begins work. Michael's checklist has the following steps for writing a sentence:

1. Think about your sentence.

2. Say your sentence out loud three times.

3. Say your sentence and tap the page where you will write the words.

4. Write the words. Tap out the sounds in each word.

Before Michael starts writing his sentence, he rehearses all the steps with his teacher.

Critical Thinking Framework

The Critical Thinking Framework helps us think through how to support students when they are struggling with grade-level content. This is not to say we should wait until after students have mastered prerequisite skills to give feedback aligned to the Critical Thinking Framework. In heterogeneous classrooms, that is a recipe to never supporting students' grade-level work. We have to be able to both shore up prerequisite skills and give appropriate feedback. Whole-group responses to missing prerequisite skills should happen in concert with the kind of feedback discussed in this section. Most of the interventions previously discussed will not interfere with the following grade-level instructional responses. Teachers can also incorporate components of the framework into reteaching or interventions, allowing students to "break it down" and "reason with evidence" even with skills intended to be mastered prior to the present grade level.

Short-Term Responses

Short-term responses usually occur during a lesson's assessment–feedback cycle or the next day in response to a previous lesson's work product, such as an exit ticket or writing sample. An effective short-term response is just that—short. Aim to deliver the feedback in 5 minutes or less, though some responses may need 10 minutes. The goal is to give students feedback as well as an opportunity to implement it. As they practice, monitor their work to see the impact of the feedback.

- **If students are making a logistical error—their papers are disorganized, work is labeled incorrectly, a direction is misread—pause the class and explicitly reset expectations.** *"While walking around, I noticed some students just filling in the blanks of the sentence starters. I want to see everyone writing out complete sentences. Use the sentence starters to help you write a complete sentence on the lines below. Watch me do the first one, and then do the next one independently."*

- **Explicitly model a skill for the class while thinking aloud.** *"Watch how I read this paragraph and summarize in my own words. Notice how I am thinking about the topic sentence and the bolded vocabulary words to include the most important ideas."*

- **Present a student-created model or exemplar.** Teachers and students work together to annotate the strong characteristics of the work: *"How did _____ solve this problem? Let's break it down. What did they do first? Next? Why did that work?"* A student could also model a specific skill or behavior for the class: *"Notice how _____ was able to put their finger on the exact sentence to back up their thinking. Let's do that together."*

- **During a discussion, highlight what students are doing as well as what they are missing.** Tell students what you are hearing and what you are not hearing in their responses. *"I hear you telling me about the beginning of the text, but to understand how the character has changed, we need to think about the entire text."*

- **After detecting a common error across the class, lead an error analysis.** Show two pieces of student work, one with a common error and one without (protect students' anonymity by labeling the samples as 1 and 2). Have students vote on which they agree with and discuss ways to improve the work. After the discussion, the teacher or students articulate a specific next step to improve student work, for example, *"When writing more than one sentence, we need to separate our sentences with a period. As I come around, I'm looking for students rereading their sentences to find places they need to add a period."*

- **Compare two examples of excellent student work.** Two student work samples may represent different ideas or strategies but both be correct. Discuss what they have in common and what they do differently. The teacher or students articulate a clear takeaway. *"While Evan used sticks and dots and Laniyah used a number line, they both broke up their numbers into 10s and 1s to add efficiently."*

In all of these short-term responses, you should use total participation techniques to engage the minds of every student, especially when a significant percentage of the class shares a common error. You can also take your instruction to the next level by strategically calling on students to explain the error and how to address it. Early discussion will likely rely on students who did not make the error, but struggling students should be called on or conferenced with so that they can demonstrate their understanding.

Long-Term Responses

Similar to long-term responses for lacking prerequisite knowledge, long-term responses to whole-class struggles with grade-level content may require adjustments to the curriculum or instructional blocks. As discussed in Chapter 5, it is important to maintain some flexibility within instructional blocks and pacing calendars so we can respond to trends in student misunderstandings. Because most elementary teachers spend the entire day with their class, some responses can be incorporated into other parts of the schedule by finding 5- to 10-minute pockets throughout the day to address misconceptions or reinforce new learning.

As you review the long-term responses, remember that some, such as academic warmups and visual scaffolds, can be implemented proactively at the beginning of a new school year or unit. Teachers and grade-level teams who already know where students tend to struggle may be able to anticipate and prevent misunderstandings.

- **Practice academic warmups at the beginning of the class to review and reinforce newly learned material.** Examples include low-stakes pop quizzes, songs and chants that review definitions or steps, and short review games.

- **Create visuals for important definitions and thinking steps.** These visual anchors should be posted in an easy-to-access location. Better yet, they can be embedded in student work materials or placed in a group's space for shared materials. *"I noticed we often forget how to set up expanded notation. As we practice, use this visual to help remind you of the parts." "As you edit this paragraph, use the capitalization chart to double-check the rules for capital letters."*

- **As a class or grade-level team, use flexible teaching days throughout or at the end of a unit to reteach an objective.** *"Even after multiple cycles of feedback, students are still struggling to write a structured paragraph. We're going to take a day to reteach the parts of a paragraph. Then we will add a flexible day next week and the week after* *to give students another opportunity to practice writing a structured paragraph."*

- **As a grade-level team, revise the curriculum to incorporate opportunities for students to practice unmastered material.** For example, in the previous unit, students struggled to describe the central message of a fiction text. Teachers can change some of the discussion and writing questions in an upcoming unit so that students can revisit the concept of a central message.

Small-Group Feedback

When to use: 4–7 students (15–25 percent of students) share an error or misunderstanding.

Rationale: The purpose of directing feedback to a small group instead of the whole group is to protect the class's practice time. When only a few students will benefit from a piece of feedback, targeting a small group allows you to address an error efficiently without disrupting others. Approaches to giving small-group feedback vary based on the type of classroom. Most single-teacher classrooms will have a different small-group system than a classroom with two teachers. A cotaught classroom may already use parallel and station teaching to target the needs of students in small groups. In a classroom with a single teacher, working in small groups requires more planning. The following short-term and long-term recommendations include suggestions for structuring small groups for solo teachers.

Teachers need to be nimble when addressing small groups of students. Some classrooms have dedicated spaces, like a U-shaped table where a few students can meet with a teacher. But not every classroom has enough space for separate whole-group and small-group locations. Sometimes teachers can push desks together or designate a table to meet with students. Other times, students may need to move to a different workspace for this strategy to work. Classrooms with a rug may be able to meet with small groups in that location.

As you reflect on ways to implement short- and long-term responses, bear in mind that small groups are most effective when they focus on one or two discrete objectives. Keep the purpose of the small group focused on a clear goal, and do not dedicate more time than is necessary to address that goal. Small groups intended to meet once or twice sometimes become permanent, which can discourage students. You can avoid this problem by building formative and summative assessments into your small-group plans. Try to disband small groups as soon as enough students master the material. If one or two students continue to struggle, they should be addressed individually.

Missing Prerequisite Knowledge

When a small group of students is missing essential prerequisite knowledge, avoid delaying the grade-level curriculum for the entire class. At the same time, maintain access to the grade-level instruction for the group of students who need support. With short- and long-term responses in place, students can master prerequisites and grade-level objectives simultaneously.

Short-Term Responses

Similar to the responses in the whole-group section, short-term responses are quick interventions to supply students with the prerequisite knowledge required to access grade-level instruction.

- **Before a lesson, preview vocabulary definitions or background knowledge with a small group of students.** This intervention can occur as students arrive in the morning, during the first few minutes of lunch, or when students complete another activity early. Teachers can also preview material with a small group while the rest of the class engages in an independent warmup activity. For example, a writing diagnostic reveals that seven students write in complete sentences but do not use ending punctuation. While other students begin their writing assignment, the teacher keeps those seven students on the rug to review the types of ending punctuation. After they practice one or two examples, the teacher sends them to their seats to begin their assignment.

- **Differentiate the worksheets completed during independent work time so that students can practice relevant skills.** For example, five students struggle to remember the upcoming decade number when counting. In the morning, they fill out worksheets that ask them to skip-count by 10s and fill in missing numbers. The students later review the work in a teacher-led small group.

Long-Term Responses

Some small groups may need sustained attention over the course of several days or weeks to address missing prerequisites. You will need to use your discretion to determine how much time to dedicate to a small group. Formatively assessing students may enable some students to graduate from the small group faster than others.

In some classes, small groups form, disband, and change so frequently that students hardly notice. Unfortunately, students may resist participating in a small group, especially if it makes them feel ostracized. Any feedback given in a small group will be for naught if students are emotionally activated against the group. When students need to meet in a small group repeatedly, consider another site for the meeting, or, if the group must meet in the same room as the rest of the class, present the small group in positive terms. Students often love being invited to a "club" or a "special meeting" with a teacher. The more often a group meets, the more necessary it is to create a positive identity for the group.

- **Assign seats to make check-ins and small-group instruction easier.** Change seat assignments frequently based on student need. For example, the teacher assigns seats according to the instructional block. At the beginning of ELA, students move to their seat assignments. While most students complete a "do now" with questions about the previous day's lesson, the ones seated at the purple table review the parts of a complete sentence and then convert fragments into complete sentences. A week later, the seat assignments change. The students at the purple table now review how to use quotation marks.

- **For students missing essential skills that require sustained practice, create a one- to two-week plan to review one skill at a time.** For instance, students who need to review all of their math facts within 10 should start with their math facts within 5. Students who struggle to differentiate between vowel sounds when spelling should first review the individual vowels. At the end of the one or two weeks, assess student progress. Progress monitoring may already be part of your school's practice under programs such as Response to Intervention. For example, a group of 3rd graders cannot skip-count by 2s, 5s, and 10s. To ensure they will be able to access the unit on multiplication, the teacher meets with them in a small group during the arrival period and the first few minutes of math. They practice skip-counting, fill in number charts, and predict patterns. They also take some practice work home to continue reviewing the skills. At the end of two weeks, the teacher gives the group a short skip-counting assessment to evaluate their progress.

Critical Thinking Framework

Students master grade-level material at different rates, especially when their levels of preparation vary. At the beginning of grade-level instruction, teachers can use the short- and long-term responses for the whole group. As a larger percentage of students demonstrate understanding of a grade-level objective, teachers will need to transition to more small-group instruction to address misconceptions and support skill development. The short- and long-term responses for whole and small groups are nearly identical. The main problem is how to efficiently meet with small groups to deliver targeted feedback. Suggestions for when and how teachers can work with small groups accompany the following responses.

Short-Term Responses

Most short-term responses are given within the lesson's assessment–feedback cycle. If a formative assessment taken after students practice a new skill reveals that the majority of the class does not require feedback, target the small group of students that does.

- **Explicitly model a skill for the small group while thinking aloud.**

- **Review a student-created exemplar with a small group.** The exemplar should demonstrate one or two characteristics you want to see in the group's independent work. Give the students clear instructions for next steps.

- **Lead the small group in an error analysis.** Students can compare an exemplar with a piece of student work that represents a common error the group makes. After analyzing both examples, you or the students articulate a crisp takeaway and next step.

Here are some logistical suggestions for working with a small group in different types of classroom spaces:

- **Dedicate a table or floor space for small-group meetings.** Make sure this space includes any necessary materials, like chart paper or a whiteboard.

- **If meeting with the whole class on the rug, keep students who need small-group support there.** Send the larger group of students to their regular seats to continue practicing or engage in another independent activity.

- **When monitoring students at their seats, put a star on the paper of students who need to meet in a small group.** Call them to the meeting location after you have determined who needs intervention versus who can continue working independently.

Long-Term Responses

Teachers and grade-level teams can plan long-term interventions for a small group of students based on summative assessment checkpoints throughout the year. As a reminder, summative assessments assess student mastery of multiple objectives. When a small group of students needs continued support on one or more grade-level objectives, the teacher may need to revise instructional blocks or curriculum plans to target the needs of the small group. However, if students are struggling with grade-level objectives because they lack the prerequisite knowledge from a previous grade, the small group should first focus on addressing those learning gaps.

Not every small-group intervention requires the teacher to meet with a small group of students for an extended period. A teacher may meet with a group to model how to use a new scaffold and then release them to fully participate in all of the class's activities. When a teacher does meet in a small group over the course of days or weeks, it's important to have set clear objectives for the group so the teacher and students can attain them and move on. The goal of any intervention is for students to eventually no longer need the intervention.

- **Based on summative assessment results, create strategic partnerships for turn-and-talks or partner work.** Students who struggled with an objective will work with a student who demonstrated understanding. For example, in 2nd grade, six students read grade-level texts accurately, but they lack prosody and phrasing. A teacher meets with these six students twice a week to practice reading in phrases and with expression. During partner reading in phonics, the teacher pairs each of the students with a fluent reader so they can see additional models.

- **Create a scaffold that students can use to support their independent work, such as a personal anchor chart, checklist, word bank, sentence starters, or number chart.** Don't offer a scaffold before students are taught how to use it. You can leverage a small-group meeting to model scaffold use for students. The goal is for students to use the scaffold with independence. For example, a group of five 3rd graders struggle to describe a character's personality traits with grade-appropriate vocabulary. The teacher creates a word bank with visual representations of positive, neutral, and negative traits. The students refer to this word bank when participating in discussions or responding to a writing prompt.

- **When you need to address the needs of two or more small groups, adapt the instructional block to include stations or parallel teaching.** In a cotaught classroom, both teachers can work with a group simultaneously. In a solo-taught classroom, the teacher can assign students to stations to complete independent tasks and meet with a small group at one of the stations. If each small group meeting lasts 20–25 minutes, a teacher can work with at least two groups in an hour-long period. For example, in a 5th grade class, nine students are still struggling to add decimals to the hundredths place, while four students are still struggling to add decimals to the tenths place. During math stations, the teacher meets with each group for 20 minutes to review examples and provide additional practice opportunities. When students move back to an independent station, they engage in a practice activity aligned to the small-group objective.

Individual Feedback

When to use: One to three students share an error or misunderstanding.

Rationale: When three or fewer students alone share an error or misunderstanding, there's no need for you to restructure the curriculum and instructional day. The needs of individual students matter, and we will discuss ways to address them here. Keep in mind that what is sustainable to create and provide for one or two students can quickly become unsustainable, if not impossible to deliver, when done for the entire class. If whole-group and small-group responses to formative and summative assessments are occurring with consistency, the vast majority of students can have their academic needs met within the classroom. Usually, individual support follows feedback cycles in the whole group and small group. Students who need individual support are the ones for whom whole- and small-group interventions did not work.

I can imagine many teachers' thoughts at this point. What if these interventions don't work? What if the student is just too far behind to catch up? I want to pause here to acknowledge that not all interventions work with every student. Moreover, it may not be possible to meet the full needs of a student within the four walls of a classroom. No matter how targeted we are in our assessment–feedback cycles, there will still be students who need more from educators who specialize in fields like speech pathology and occupational therapy. In these situations, contact the school's special education department about a Response to Intervention (RTI) plan or an evaluation for an IEP.

If a student already has an IEP, read it carefully to understand their individual goals and mandated interventions. This doesn't mean we should not give students with IEPs grade-level work, nor should we exempt them from the normal assessment and feedback cycles within the classroom. An IEP does not prevent a student from learning and mastering grade-level skills, but that student may require additional support before or during instruction to be successful, or may have a different rate of growth than other students. Once again, this is not an excuse to deny students with special needs grade-level instruction, but it does mean we may have to make sensible adjustments.

Missing Prerequisite Knowledge

Diagnostic assessments at the beginning of the year will help you determine what knowledge gaps your students have. We can make a number of strategic whole-group and small-group plans to address these gaps, but we still need to address outliers. Just because only one student in the class struggles with place value doesn't mean they don't get to learn place value. Nor does it mean that the entire class needs to review an objective they already mastered.

Teachers can and should leverage small-group times to meet with an individual or pair who share a common goal, especially when that additional instruction will guarantee access to the grade-level curriculum. As suggested for small groups, teachers can teach individual students how to support their classwork with scaffolds such as personal anchor charts, checklists, word banks, number charts, sentence starters, and more. Some of these interventions may even be mandated for students with a Section 504 plan or IEP.

However, it isn't always in a student's interest to give them every available scaffold, nor is it necessary to maintain those scaffolds for an extended period of time. When we put a scaffold in place, we need to plan for how and when to gradually release students from the support. Our ultimate goal is to instill academic independence rather than dependence on adults.

As you choose an appropriate short-term or long-term response to support individual students, consider the following:

- Based on diagnostic assessments, what are the specific prerequisites the student needs? Is it counting to 120? Reading CVC words? Writing a complete sentence? In the same way you use the assessment–feedback cycle to target one or two discrete objectives with whole and small groups, you should identify objectives for individuals. Sometimes teachers define a student by a long list of deficits that feels impossible to address. To counter these feelings of helplessness, remain clear-eyed and tethered to reality—and then choose a place to start.

- How will teaching teams track the individual's progress toward each objective?

When planning a sequence of objectives to address with an individual, consider how the objectives align with the grade-level curriculum. If a student is solidifying their counting skills within 1,000 as well as rounding numbers to the nearest tenth, reflect on which objective better serves the student during a unit on multidigit addition and subtraction.

- Can the intervention be done without singling out the student? Many supports, such as adjusted writing paper, sentence starters, personal checklists, and number charts, can be implemented without drawing undue attention to the student.

- If the individual needs an intervention in a separate location, can it happen within the context of a small group? How can you reduce transition time?

Critical Thinking Framework

When an individual student needs additional support with the grade-level content, most interventions can be nearly invisible. The Critical Thinking Framework can help us think through how and when to deliver high-quality feedback to students, but first we need to establish effective routines such as the following:

- Expectations for equal participation in turn-and-talks, cold calls, and independent work periods are communicated to students from the beginning of the year.

- Students have easy access to all materials they need, which usually requires well-organized workspaces.

- Seat assignments and workspaces around the room allow the teacher to easily circulate and monitor student work.

- Lesson preparation includes the teacher internalizing the current performance of the class based on prior diagnostics and summative and formative assessments and uses this information to anticipate who in the class may need additional support.

These routines are a few of the most essential, but others can also be beneficial.

What can individual feedback look and sound like? Most teachers are familiar with the following scenario:

> The teacher circulates while students practice and notices a student making an error. The teacher pauses the student and says, "I can see you are doing _____ well. Go back and double-check _____" or "Let me show you how to do this again."

Of course, other responses are possible, but most quick feedback looks like this. Still, many teachers struggle to give quick feedback, and it doesn't always target what students need. Sometimes teachers find themselves occupied with one student without ever having time to check in on anyone else. For this reason, I recommend avoiding individual feedback at the beginning of a formative assessment cycle, unless the student misunderstood the task. Teachers need to circulate and monitor every student first. Usually, we can more efficiently address misunderstandings through whole-group and small-group responses. When individuals require feedback, we need strategies to offer targeted feedback without disrupting the flow of the class.

Figure 6.3 describes ways teachers can respond to common student errors and misconceptions. The Critical Thinking Framework helps organize the types of errors teachers may see and offers suggestions for feedback, but it cannot replace the actual preparation work covered in Chapter 3. High-quality feedback relies on high-quality preparation. Depending on teacher preparation and classroom context, the suggested responses can occur in the short term (on the same day or the next) or in the long term (over the course of several days and weeks). The responses range from feedback given directly to the student in the moment to adjustments implemented over several lessons.

Conclusion

This chapter is all about the nitty-gritty—how can teachers make strategic decisions to propel the learning of every student in their class? The answer isn't always to approach individual students with feedback but, rather, to look for trends across a class. When individuals do need feedback, teachers can choose from a range of supports and interventions that need not disrupt the overall flow of a class.

FIGURE 6.3

Responses to Student Errors Guided by the Critical Thinking Framework

Critical Thinking Framework Component	Student Errors	Teacher Responses
Say it in your own words	Student can repeat a definition but not explain it in their own words or apply it in context.	Create and maintain a bulletin board of taught vocabulary. Routinely review and practice the vocabulary represented on the board. Ask students to reread definitions to help them review and revise their work. For example, say, "It looks like you are confusing the landforms canyon and coast. Go reread the definitions. When you come back, look at the pictures and determine which word applies." During class discussions and independent practice, circulate or call on the student to ensure they receive more practice with the concept.
Break it down	Student cannot apply all the steps of a procedure. Student cannot explain how one step is connected to another. Student applies an incorrect procedure because they misunderstand the task.	Refer the student to a visual or personal checklist. Prompt, "How do we start? What's next? Then?" Model the thinking process aloud, pausing between steps: "Notice what I'm doing now. I see _____ and _____, which makes me think _____." During teacher modeling, pause at critical junctures to ask the student, "How should I respond in this situation?" Provide a written example students can refer to. For example, say, "You skipped Step 2. Go back to Step 1 and follow the directions in Step 2" while indicating the steps on a printed checklist. Reread the prompt. Ask, "What is this asking us to do? I notice you thought to apply _____ here. Why doesn't that make sense?"
Look for structure	Student misidentifies a question type due to surface-level characteristics. Student draws an incorrect analogy.	Ask the student, "What do you know? What do you not know? What's a method for figuring out what you don't know?" Say, "You're responding to this question as if it were asking _____. But it is actually asking _____."

Critical Thinking Framework Component	Student Errors	Teacher Responses
Look for structure —(continued)	Student applies the same idea or strategy irrespective of the question. Student does not notice similarities between tasks.	Show the student an example problem and ask, "What's similar between these examples? How should you respond to this question?" Post or share metacognitive thinking steps, for example, "When we approach a task like _____, we have to ask ourselves _____ and _____. Start at the beginning." Suggest, "Use this graphic organizer to jot down your answers to these smaller questions first."
Notice gaps and inconsistencies	Student struggles to formulate questions. Student is unable to notice differences between examples. Student struggles to revise their own work when analyzing a model or referring to a checklist.	Provide question stems. Model formulating a question before asking the student to do so. Ask, "Is every step the same? Which step is different? Point to the step that is different." Model for the student, saying, for example, "Watch me use the checklist for your first two sentences. Notice how I'm going slowly, word for word. Right away, I see that this word at the start of the sentence needs a capital."
Reason with evidence	Student provides no evidence. Student offers confused or inaccurate evidence. Student's citation of evidence is limited. Student provides evidence but fails to explain or justify it.	Prompt student to add evidence: "What makes you think that?" In a text, ask the student to put their finger on the sentence or page that supports their idea. Provide criteria for strong evidence. Say, "Your evidence is _____, but it doesn't have _____. How can we improve your evidence?" Say, "This is interesting evidence. Can you explain to me why it's important?"

All of the examples in this chapter are flexible. Teachers require a range of options to nimbly respond to the needs of their class, especially since they cannot plan for every contingency. Teachers who teach the same grade for several years will see a number of similarities across cohorts, but they will also notice key differences in how to best respond and support different groups. Some cohorts will have weak prerequisite knowledge in one area but not another, while some years the cohort needs very little remediation but struggles with grade-level content.

Chapter 6 Key Points

- Preparation is critical for high-quality feedback.

- Teachers can use the process explained in Chapter 3 to prepare for content instruction, especially in the areas where students may struggle.

- Diagnostic and summative assessments can highlight areas of focus for the whole class, a small group of students, and individuals.

- Teachers should track students during formative assessment periods to determine the kind of feedback they need.

- Teachers should provide whole-group feedback when a third or more of the class share an error or misunderstanding.

- Small-group and individual feedback should focus on one or two discrete objectives.

- All examples and suggestions for feedback are flexible—they can and should be revised and applied according to the teacher's judgment about their students and specific context.

7 FOSTERING AN INTELLECTUAL COMMUNITY THROUGHOUT THE YEAR

In the K–12 continuum, elementary school stands apart. Often until 5th grade (and sometimes even into middle school), students learn together in a single community of 20–30 people. In such a community, academics are not easily dissociated from the social life of the classroom. Relationships between teachers and students, as well as among students themselves, can strengthen or thwart the academic purposes of school. Yet we should not reduce relationships and community to a simple transaction: fuzzy-wuzzy feelings in exchange for good learning behavior. Fostering meaningful classroom relationships is an end in itself, providing opportunities for adults to model care, boundaries, fairness, and emotional constancy. Elementary teachers spend hours a day with their students, and in that time, they demonstrate multitudinous ways of acting in the world for their students.

Academics cannot be the sole focus of a book about critical thinking in elementary school. From the moment students enter their classrooms, elementary teachers are crafting environments. These environments set the tone for the daily experiences of students—experiences that may last anywhere from six to nine hours a day. Teachers interested in creating opportunities for deep thinking and questioning should avoid thinking about the classroom as silos of content disciplines. Although the students may change topics throughout the day, they sit in the same chairs and on the same rug in the same classroom. And throughout the day, whether the appointed moment serves academics or leisure, children talk to one another. And where there is talk, there is an opportunity for *analysis, evaluation,* and *judgment*—in other words, an opportunity for critical thinking.

Opportunities abound to extend and deepen thinking outside core academic subjects. These opportunities can allow teachers and students to build meaningful relationships, engage in reflection, and even develop greater knowledge about the world. In this chapter, I share how I think about building a classroom community throughout the year, one where students and teachers bring their authentic hearts and minds. I also emphasize ways to foster an intellectual community, even when academics are not the focus. The primary principles of this approach are the following:

- Tell the story of your class.

- Celebrate struggle.

- Model intellectual honesty.

- Normalize disagreement and multiple perspectives with meaningful talk.

Similar to other chapters, this one provides guidelines to think through your own classroom as well as suggestions to try. Nothing in this chapter is prescriptive; rather, my suggestions are inspired by hard-won lessons from a decade of classroom teaching. I do not pretend to manage every scenario and situation perfectly in my own classes. In fact, I share difficult and at times embarrassing stories from my own experiences. Even a decade's worth of teaching could never prepare me for the cacophonous array of personalities found in young children; discovering their idiosyncrasies and personal quirks is one of the true joys of working in an elementary school. The principles I describe here are elastic enough to adapt to most groups, even the most unexpected and unique. I hope these experiences illuminate better ways to be in community with children, as well as better ways to simply be in community.

Tell the Story of Your Class

In my first weeks of teaching, nothing went well. Not a single thing. Someone might say there had to be something tiny that went well. Otherwise, how could I possibly stay in teaching? Fortunately, my tolerance for abject failure is high.

I recall a well-meaning coach standing on the corner of the rug as my 2nd graders ignored everything I said. They talked and giggled with one another; they paid no mind to me. I gave the coach a look of total desperation. She started whispering some things for me to say, such as "These choices make it seem like you don't value your education or think learning is important."

I repeated them.

Like most teachers, I replay my lowest moments again and again. I wish I could go back in time and respond, "I don't think that will work. Maybe there's something else?" At the time, as a true novice, I depended on the support and advice available to me. Even though I now know how to respond in that situation, it took years of practice.

Unfortunately, I have heard these exact words uttered in every school I have worked in since. It's quite sad to consider how prevalent certain phrases remain. When children are disruptive or chatty, many adults respond by telling them that they must not like learning or they must not care about school. Sometimes the students go silent, as if something extremely solemn has just been declared. But sometimes they respond the way my students did in those first weeks: they giggle. Either way, even when the words appear to yield a positive response, the effect is typically short-lived.

My poor response then was the beginning of many poor responses. In my first years, I never took the time to think critically and make a well-reasoned choice about the kind of classroom I wanted. I lacked the expertise to sort through the number of high-stakes decisions I needed to make. I almost never set clear expectations with my students; even when I did, they were not high expectations. I cared more about observable behaviors than what was happening in their minds, and I did not spend time creating routines to help me hear or see their ideas. I certainly did not talk about our hopes and dreams for the school year or the type of classroom we would like to share together. I thought silence was a positive reflection on my management rather than a prerequisite for focus; classroom silence became a battleground of control rather than an active ingredient to foster a calm environment for thinking.

The classroom environment is of the utmost importance for educators pursuing ambitious academic outcomes. Classroom community requires the same careful planning and attention to detail as any curriculum vision or formative assessment cycle. Children need safe, warm, structured environments in order to try new things, ask questions, share ideas with others, receive feedback and criticism, and engage in revision. This is hard, emotionally activating work for children, and they need the support of responsible adults. Beyond academics, students are dealing with friendships formed and broken, a growing sense of ego in the games played at recess, and anxieties about assigned seats and partners. As every elementary teacher knows, the tangle of needs and interests in the classroom must be scrupulously combed through and woven together. The art of crafting such an environment begins with the power of the teacher's voice.

Later in my career, when I took time to reflect and plan for my ideal classroom environment, I realized I had failed to comprehend the power of the teacher's voice. When I did use my voice during those initial years, it was too frequently to tell my students a sad story about themselves, one where they did not listen or care about our time in the classroom. Sometimes it was a story of my authority and their lack of respect for it. It almost always painted me, the adult, as a victim and the students as antagonists. The story became truer each time I told it. Yes, I had wonderful moments when I saw real connections forged and progress made, but I did not shine a light on these moments or acknowledge their importance often enough. The emotions associated with positive events were ephemeral, while the emotions of negative events took on a toxic potency. At the time, I believed if I were to tally the sums of negative and positive, negative would win the day. Now I know there is almost always a different story available.

Teachers are the narrators of their classroom's story. Whether we like it or not, our voices are the loudest in the room; it is a physical fact. While we hope to teach children to lean in and hear one another, they usually come to school ready first to listen to teachers. This is a serious responsibility. As philosopher Bertrand Russell (1916) points out in his provocative essay on education, authority is an unavoidable aspect of teaching. The way teachers choose to use authority matters significantly, and it must be infused with a spirit of reverence for the dignity of the children in our classrooms. When we tell the story of our classrooms, even classrooms full of trials and tribulations, we can choose to tell one full of progress and aspiration.

As a teacher, it does not always seem possible to be the author of your own story, much less the story of the collective group. Add vague words like *reverence* to the mix, and quite a few teachers will find their eyes rolling to the back of their heads. In my first years of teaching, I would have denied having any hand in authoring the story of my class. As I vacillated between demanding absolute control and surrendering responsibility, I scorned the concept of a happy, calm classroom as utopian malarkey. I usually blamed larger systems for my own struggles to build a warm and consistent community. Even though these larger systems certainly contributed to very real difficulties—chaotic schedules and school settings, inadequate preparation, extreme oversight and accountability from administration, food and housing insecurity, pervasive racism and discrimination experienced by students in the school and wider communities—they did not and could not explain away all the challenges I faced. To show reverence for my students, I had to first and foremost think about how to cultivate a community. More important, I had to take responsibility for my essential role in creating that community.

The delicate balance of authority and reverence is a difficult one, and I won't pretend otherwise. Teachers must be serious about wielding authority not because they want to exert control but, rather, so they can set parameters and goals for their students that matter—even if students don't realize it. For the youngest children, negotiating their needs and wants with the needs and wants of several other children is not a regular experience before they enter school. Learning to share space with other bodies can be uncomfortable, if not downright irritating, for children, and they may not have the tools or words to cope in every new situation. This is where the teacher plays a key role. By communicating expectations and boundaries, as well as clear reasons and rationales, we invite students to understand a new kind of environment in a safe and supported way. From one perspective, we might see parallels with our earlier discussions of academic learning. If we expect students to be able to deal with difficult emotions and solve problems with one another, they need to be equipped with the knowledge and skills to handle that situation. We can use our authority as the leading voice in the room to explicitly teach them to students—a foundation for later independence.

Unlike secondary teachers, who teach several different groups of students, elementary teachers can cultivate a community with a smaller group of students with norms and values that persist the entire school year. While whole schools share a mission and set of values across classrooms, it is the special work of classroom teachers to realize that vision in the daily experiences of their students. These values and norms are truly visible in the daily, seemingly minor interactions between the teacher and students. When we have total clarity about the type of community we want to create—one of mutual respect, openness to new ideas, and resilience in response to challenge—we can recognize even the smallest moments that make that community a living reality.

To tell the story of our class, we must first ensure we actually have a clear vision. Platitudes are not enough. For too many teachers, beautifully worded slogans are the only advice they ever receive about classroom culture. The failure to build positive classroom communities is usually due to a lack of specificity in the vision—broad statements need to be replaced by concrete descriptions. Many schools help classroom teachers in this work by stipulating the expected behaviors, habits, and mindsets expected from all students within a school. Not every school provides this clarity to teachers, and some only provide it in part. No matter where your individual school lands on this spectrum, you should take the time to answer the following questions, preferably in writing:

- What are the classroom expectations that will ensure every student can learn?

- What are the mindsets and habits I want to help my students develop?

- How can I explain these expectations, mindsets, and habits in simple, easy-to-remember language?

- How will I respond to difficult behaviors and situations? How can I respond in a way that is consistent with the vision of my classroom?

- Are these expectations sustainable? Will I still be able to maintain them in April or May?

The last question is an important one. If a routine or classroom expectation is too complex or onerous to enforce, then it is unlikely to last the entire year. If I want to talk to my students about showing care in their work as well as in relationships with others, do I have a way of presenting and reinforcing these ideas that can persist throughout the year? There is nothing wrong with dismissing an ineffective procedure or revising an expectation, but students notice a lack of consistency. Consistency builds trust, but it also allows the teacher to guide students toward more independence. We know that when information is stored in long-term memory, the working memory can focus on increasingly complex tasks. This same principle applies to routines and procedures. If students have to expend mental bandwidth on tracking inconsistent expectations, they are less likely to become independent. As students understand the expectations of the classroom, from how they should treat one another to how they handle disagreements, the teacher's voice can withdraw more to the background to allow students more autonomy.

Once we have a clear vision of the behaviors, mindsets, and habits that matter, we can explain them to students. It is insufficient to explain expectations to students just once. Students benefit from revisiting expectations multiple times, at the beginning of the school year and beyond. But it is also important that students experience more than just listening to what their teacher tells them; they also need to see demonstrations of the vision in their actual classroom experiences. We can help this process by observing students carefully to see how the vision comes to life in big and small moments. When these moments occur, we should use our voice to highlight them for others, especially the aspects that we want students to emulate. The teacher's voice acts like a spotlight: it indicates to students what is important enough to pay attention to. When we use our voice to spotlight positive moments—a student steps aside to let someone else by; two students reach a compromise about what game to play; a student, stuck on a question, uses a classroom resource to get started—we emphasize the community's shared values.

These special moments are usually small, and highlighting them does not need to be a huge production; in fact, it can be done in less than 30 seconds.

Let's say a class has talked about the importance of listening closely to others. A teacher can highlight any number of moments, academic and nonacademic, to reinforce this community norm. Perhaps a student decided to try a new game at recess after listening to a friend's explanation, or at lunch one child listened to another child's story and asked follow-up questions. A teacher need only pause the class for a brief moment and say, "We've been talking about listening to one another closely, and I wanted to share something marvelous I saw during snack today. All the kids were sharing their favorite TV show. When Violet heard of a show she had not heard of before, she asked the other kids questions to learn more. That showed she was interested in what others had to say, and she asked questions to better understand. What an excellent example of listening!"

As we model praise in these small moments, students learn behaviors and mindsets they can incorporate into their own lives. Students also learn how to share compliments and praise themselves. We can create classroom traditions and rituals where students recognize one another for displaying shared values or other positive contributions to the classroom community. In classes where these practices are consistently part of the classroom life, students may spontaneously notice and compliment one another. I once saw a student shoot their hand in the air after returning from recess to share how another child helped them find a lost sweater. They were grateful, and they wanted everyone to know about the other child's kindness: "They helped me even though they didn't have to!"

Highlighting and narrating the positive moments in a classroom matters. Teachers should find several opportunities every day to do so. But the greater challenge is telling the story of your class in the not-positive moments, when an expectation is not met or a boundary is disregarded. What is an educator to do then? Responses to misbehavior often rely on school policies, but I have a few specific recommendations in keeping with this section's theme:

- **Do not tell everyone.** Most misbehavior is individual or involves only a few students. Do not let the story of the one or the few become the story of the class. As much as possible, address these misbehaviors out of the public eye.

- **Respond based on facts, not emotions.** Sometimes a student will approach you to say someone was bullying them, but further conversations reveal that the interaction was more complicated than that one initial statement implied. As a teacher, I have to remind myself that the first story I hear is not always the correct one, and I do not want to model making assumptions or jumping to conclusions. Gather the facts first and then respond.

- **Keep small problems small.** The response to misbehavior should be logical and proportional, and most behaviors are small. A student calling out does not merit a whole-class lecture, nor does it require a large consequence. Based on the incident and school context, a quick anonymous reminder or nonverbal look will suffice to stop the disruption. Remember, a big response from the teacher signals to the whole class that something important is going on. When a teacher stops teaching fractions to call out a student publicly for tapping their pencil or slouching, they are sending the implicit message that the small behavior of one student is more important than the learning of all the others. We should prepare an arsenal of responses—proximity, nonverbal gestures, whispers—to keep small problems small.

- **Some problems are not small.** Let's say a hurtful thing was said or someone was hit. As discussed above, these problems do not need to be addressed publicly in front of a class unless there was a whole-class impact that forces a larger conversation. Moreover, the response to the behavior should be logical and proportional, and teachers should follow the guidance of their schools in planning an appropriate response. In most situations, teachers will at some point engage in a conversation with the student to explain a consequence or next step. In this conversation, teachers have a unique opportunity to tell the story of their class. It is important to communicate care while also reinforcing community expectations. Such an interaction could sound like one of the following responses:
  - "Taking responsibility for a mistake is hard and doesn't feel good, but it is also a chance for us to learn and do better moving forward."

- "In our class, we reflect on what we do well and how we can improve. This is an opportunity for reflection."
- "One mistake doesn't define you. What you do next is what matters the most."
- "The reason we're talking about honesty right now is because honesty allows us to trust one another. You are an important part of this community, and we can use this opportunity to rebuild trust."
- "Apologizing isn't easy, but it lets someone know that you care and you won't do it again. Let's talk about what a good apology is and what it isn't."
- "Our class cares about keeping the room clean for everyone who uses it, so let's clean this up."

Clarity of vision equips teachers to know the behaviors, mindsets, and habits that matter in their community. With this knowledge, we can invite students into our vision and make genuine connections to their lives. As we support this process by providing transparent explanations of expectations and the rationale behind them, we can observe the vision coming to life in the classroom. When magnificent moments of kindness or resilience occur, we teachers should not keep them to ourselves—we need to use our spotlight voice to tell everyone!

Although sharing our classroom narrative is powerful, we need to be thoughtful practitioners of the technique; in particular, teachers must make sure they are shining a spotlight on authentic examples. A student who repeatedly treats others unkindly should be recognized when they demonstrate improvement, such as during the 30-second spotlights described above. But well-meaning educators sometimes bestow awards on students not because they deserve the recognition but, rather, to build up the students' self-esteem or encourage a correction in their behavior. These good intentions can backfire and undermine critical trust between teachers and students. When students see overwhelming praise given without merit, the praise and the praise-giver both lose credibility. This is true even with the youngest students. Children are laser-focused on matters of justice. They will buy into inspirational moments as long as they seem fair and concrete, but they will withdraw their support when adults cross the threshold into meaningless compliments untethered from reality.

Celebrate Struggle

Most schools fashion a unique set of values and traits to impart to their students. International Baccalaureate schools use Learner Profiles, while other schools use a list of adjectives, sometimes with catchy acronyms, to describe the characteristics the school or community values most. I argue that we should add an atypical value to this list, one I have witnessed again and again in every class no matter the age or content taught: *struggle*. Not to be confused with buzz phrases like "productive struggle," *struggle* here refers to an ethos of revision and continuous improvement, a sense of humility and curiosity when tackling a big, wide world full of novel challenges, and even a belief in the worthiness of doing hard things. This definition includes many character traits found in school acronyms, but they are branches sharing a common tree trunk: a positive outlook and relationship with the learning process, a process that inevitably includes struggle. Children and adults alike seek the comfort of certainty and the protection of always being right, though the learning process, done correctly, often undermines our certainty and revokes such protection.

A particularly perspicacious student of mine spent most of the school year mastering every mathematics standard within a few days of it being taught. Usually, they enjoyed challenges, and they worked with the confidence of someone who knew they could succeed at figuring out most problems if given enough time. When we worked on three-digit subtraction problems, the student repeatedly paused at problems like $601 - 237$. Unsure of what to do when they couldn't regroup from a 0, they worked the problem using direct modeling strategies (i.e., they solved it by drawing a place value representation of flats, sticks, and dots). However, when using an algorithmic representation, they remained stumped. They declared to me that this problem was "wrong" because they couldn't get one of the strategies to work. I gently but firmly told them the algorithm did work. Frustrated, they needed to take a few minutes to calm down before analyzing an example with me.

After several rounds of examples and discussion, this student remained stumped. Accustomed to a much faster learning process, they were exasperated when they could not readily master the new skill. Throughout, I corrected the student and still required them to practice the algorithm, although they attempted to avoid it by turning to easier direct modeling strategies. They were unsettled by the struggle, but the task at hand—regrouping a larger number to subtract a smaller number—was within their capacity to understand. At no point did I dismiss this student's authentic emotional reaction. I sought to find the tricky balance between emotional security and warm accountability. They needed to feel seen but also be nudged to stick with it. I told them with no uncertainty that they were capable, despite experiencing challenge so far; with more examples and deliberate practice, they could do it. This response acknowledged the hard work ahead as well as a belief in their ability to reach high expectations.

After several more examples, a small-group reteach, and many more clarifying questions, the eureka moment occurred: "Oh, I get it! I'm regrouping bigger and bigger numbers until I have enough to subtract." Invigorated with this new knowledge, the student begged to share and model for the rest of the class. When they overheard another student experiencing the same struggle, they eagerly offered to talk them through the steps. When sharing reflections and shout-outs during the class's closing circle, an end-of-day ritual, I told the class the student's story.

Struggle, mistakes, risk taking—these can be emotionally activating for students. Students will not adopt a positive orientation toward struggle without explicit instruction and support from their teachers. Teachers can and should teach students ways to grapple with struggle and mistakes; some suggestions are presented in Figure 7.1, along with useful books to share with elementary students. It is helpful to do these activities at the beginning of the year, but they can also be infused throughout the later months. Lessons grounded in rich texts and read-alouds provide ample fodder for conversation and reflection. Students may also benefit from acting out scenarios to help them plan ways to respond to difficult moments.

FIGURE 7.1

Grappling with Struggle: Scenarios and Read-Alouds

Student Scenarios	• Ava loves math. It's usually her best subject. But today she can't seem to solve the word problem given to the class. She feels a burning inside of her because she's embarrassed. She doesn't want anyone to find out she doesn't understand how to solve the problem. What is some advice we can give to Ava?
	• Jaden has been really focused on getting all of his ideas down in writing. When his teacher comes by, she tells him to read the first couple sentences aloud. When he does, he realizes none of the sentences make any sense! He knows he has to start over and redo the sentences, but he feels disappointed because he already did so much work. What are some positive phrases Jaden can tell himself at this moment? If you were a friend of Jaden's sitting nearby, what is something you could say to him to be supportive?
Suggested Read-Alouds	• *The Dot* by Peter H. Reynolds
	• *Ish* by Peter H. Reynolds
	• *Giraffes Can't Dance* by Giles Andreae
	• *The Girl Who Never Made Mistakes* by Mark Pett and Gary Rubinstein
	• *Ada Twist, Scientist* by Andrea Beaty
	• *Your Fantastic Elastic Brain* by JoAnn Deak
	• *After the Fall: How Humpty Dumpty Got Back Up Again* by Dan Santat

Model Norms of Intellectual Honesty

Whether they like it or not, teachers model behavior norms for students. Even though adults say they want children to resolve their conflicts calmly, listen to understand, and make coherent arguments to support their points, they do not always hold themselves to the same standards. When students see adults inconsistently apply codes of conduct, they learn that behavioral norms do not have intrinsic value; instead, they learn that adults use rules to control rather than teach.

Every space has some set of norms that govern behavior within that space. Libraries, restaurants, public parks, movie theaters—all of these places require certain behaviors to ensure everyone can use and share the space. Schools are no different. Not only should schools make all expectations for students transparent, but the adults responsible for enforcing these expectations should also forthrightly communicate with students the way the adults follow or depart from these norms. For example, teachers should explain to students that they may need to talk to other adults during a fire drill to ensure everyone is accounted for. Even though everyone is expected to transition quickly and silently during an emergency procedure, expectations will differ for those with other responsibilities. The same principle applies to the instructional parts of the day. Teachers frequently make mistakes—they misspeak, or change their mind, or do something incorrectly. When these moments occur, teachers should admit their mistakes or think aloud when they revise an idea. These moments allow the teacher to model emotional constancy in the response to their own errors, which gives children a template for how they can approach similar situations.

Teachers also model intellectual honesty when they plainly admit that they either do not know an answer or are unsure of their opinion. For example, when students ask me what I think about uniforms, I say something along the lines of "I grew up wearing uniforms and I hated it. I didn't think the clothes were very comfortable and I found it constricting. Now, as a teacher, I see that it helps families not worry as much about their child's clothes, and I notice that at schools without uniforms, sometimes kids feel embarrassed if their family can't afford the clothes other kids have. But I also don't like it if kids get in trouble when their uniforms aren't perfect. I think there are pros and cons to uniforms, and I'm still making up my mind about it." As adults, we often try to smooth out the wrinkles in our explanations to students, but it is perfectly adequate to say something along the lines of "It's complicated." Demonstrating comfort with uncertainty normalizes having nuanced, evolving opinions. Being unsure doesn't mean not having anything to say about a topic; it might actually mean there is more to say, and acknowledging that fact can be the beginning of a great conversation.

When the classroom culture allows for nuance and uncertainty, students learn how to seek understanding. Critical thinking is often framed as engaging in back-and-forth arguments, where one party seeks to critique and undo the position of another. Although there is a time and place for healthy debate, debate and critique alone are insufficient—the goal of critical thinking is to create the conditions for dialogue. This means teaching students to show respect for others' ideas and to listen for understanding first, even when they disagree. In an environment where they feel safe to take risks, students can disagree.

To help students attain that goal, we create norms and shared understanding around struggle, disagreement, and revision that might sound like the following:

- "We'll never get better at anything if we don't try something new and hard. That means things will be messy at first, or even for a while! That's because when we first learn how to do something, we make a ton of mistakes. This is called *struggle*, and it's part of the learning process."

- "There are some things that are easy to agree on, like 1 + 1 is 2 or the letter *B* makes the "bih" sound. But there are some things that are a lot harder for people to agree on, like whether it's ever OK to tell a lie or what the lesson of a story is. Sometimes people disagree when there are many right answers or when the right answer isn't totally clear. Just because we disagree doesn't mean we can't be persuaded to change our minds or that we can't learn something from someone we disagree with."

- "Sometimes we really think something is true or we handled a problem the right way or we really understood something. But then we hear ideas from other people, and all of a sudden we realize we were only partially right or we weren't right at all. When we *revise*, we change something to make it better. We could revise our thinking or revise our work or revise our opinions. Sometimes we just revise little things; other times, we have to revise everything. When we revise, in big and little ways, we can improve."

Meaningful Talk

Dialogue plays an essential role in the academic learning process, but teachers can facilitate meaningful talk throughout the day. Elementary school teachers enjoy the opportunity to stay with one group of students throughout the year, which allows rich social connections to develop. Some of the most difficult and important lessons and discussions occur during or after transitions or during a celebration, and certainly many conversations can be had reflecting on the challenges that come up during recess.

Most elementary classrooms have a morning meeting—a short time at the beginning of the day where kids can build community with one another. While these periods often address the schedule or attendance, they also afford a unique opportunity for meaningful talk. During morning meetings, teachers can facilitate students discussing topics of high interest or meaning to them. They can also problem-solve difficult moments emerging in the classroom, such as peer conflicts.

Much like other academic practices, meaningful talk needs to be explicitly modeled and practiced. Some schools call these norms "accountable talk" or "habits of discussion." I prefer to call it what it is: talking. Learning how to talk in different settings and shifting norms is a crucial skill. I tell students we are going to talk to one another or have a discussion. I avoid using too much jargon. Based on what we know about working memory, I want to avoid bogging down students in too much technical language, which prevents them from focusing on the thinking and talking. That said, I have a few nonnegotiables:

- Speak in complete sentences.

- Look at the person speaking or the person(s) you're speaking to.

- Stay on topic.

Speaking in complete sentences reinforces expressing complete thoughts, which also supports that skill in writing. When people engage in a discussion with one another, they don't stare out the window or turn their backs. Moreover, when students speak, I want them to speak not directly to me but to their classmates. Sometimes I will even step to the side or to the back of the room during a discussion to make it more difficult for the students to direct their speech to me. The purpose of sharing their ideas is not to get an immediate stamp of approval from me or determine whether they are on the right track based on my body language. Right or wrong, children need to learn to express themselves without looking to adult authority figures as a crutch.

Some teachers and schools require sentence stems and gestures beyond what is described here. These can work well, especially at the beginning of the year, but I try to move students away from them as soon as I can to avoid overly formulaic phrasing. Explicit ways of speaking are helpful to young students, but sometimes children will contort their ideas to fit a particular phrase or sentence structure. When I see this happening, I offer students other ways of expressing themselves. As a teacher, you can model expressing your ideas with different syntax. Remember, the teacher's voice is a powerful tool. Every time you speak or act, you are modeling something to students. Intentionally varying your sentence structure and vocabulary gives students other templates for how they can speak.

When teaching meaningful talk, provide students with examples and nonexamples. Such instruction might sound like this:

Teacher: Today we're going to share our opinions about the play materials we have at recess. Before we do that, it's important that we stay on topic when we share our ideas. For example, I might say, "I really like hula hoops during recess. They are great if you don't want to play tag or run around." That's staying on topic, because I am talking about the materials we have at recess and explaining my opinion about them.

But what if I said this instead? "I like the chalk, but chalk is only my third favorite art material. My favorite art material is paint. I actually did a lot of painting last weekend." Why is that not on topic?

Student: It kinda starts on topic, but you don't really explain your opinion about the recess materials. You just kinda go off and talk about yourself. It doesn't have anything to do with the topic.

These examples and nonexamples provide students with clear models of what to do and what not to do. Once students understand the norms and expectations, they can go through feedback cycles where they practice and reflect on their talk. Teachers can also create structures for equitable participation during small-group and whole-group discussions such as the following:

- Track the number of students sharing the same or different viewpoint.

- Track how many times each student participates.

- Encourage older students to self-monitor their participation by using "talking chips" or keeping a personal tally chart.

In keeping with the ethos of struggle and continuous improvement, we can use our spotlight voices to celebrate moments when a student changes their mind or revises their thinking. We may highlight a moment where the students do not agree but continue the conversation and listen carefully to one another. Through this process, we are normalizing disagreement and multiple perspectives. In this setting, changing one's mind or speaking up to disagree are not high-risk actions.

Make Talk Relevant

Whether in the context of morning meeting or another time of day reserved for community building and discussion, teachers can provide space for students to explore topics and questions relevant to their own experiences. (This kind of opportunity should also be carefully planned and integrated into the curriculum.) Students can analyze and evaluate problems in the classroom, issues within the school, and current events.

Analyze and Evaluate Problems in the Classroom

A former coteacher introduced me to "open discussion." This was a time set aside for students to select any topic they wanted to discuss, including issues they saw arising in class. During one such discussion, the students shared a concern. The classroom had a system known as "equity sticks." These were craft sticks bearing the name of every student in the class. We used them to randomly select students for different jobs or to respond to questions. The students noticed that once we selected someone's name, we returned the stick to the jar. This meant that some students ended up chosen more often than others, which seemed unfair. We discussed a new system to implement.

Although this problem seems small, it meant a lot to the kids. Not addressing it would disinvest them from the system created to support their learning. They also got to advocate for themselves and participate in finding a solution.

Discuss Issues Within the School

Every week, snacks were dropped off for my 2nd graders. Week after week, the snack remained the same: pretzels. At first, the students happily ate the pretzels provided. As the weeks went on, they started to grumble. Months into the school year, the students started protesting, "Pretzels again?! Is there nothing else?"

During one snack time, when discontent had reached a rolling boil, the class discussed ways to communicate our feedback. We talked about who made decisions when ordering snacks and why they may currently order pretzels rather than a more desirable snack. Inspired, a few students used their new paragraph- and essay-writing skills to plan and compose a letter advocating for different snacks.

Connect to Current Events

While a kindergartner and 5th grader likely will not share the same knowledge of or interest in current events, kids naturally notice what adults are discussing or what appears on television. They often bring questions and curiosities to the classroom. Sometimes the school curriculum provides some answers, but today's elementary schools do not necessarily teach the basic geography, social studies, and science that students need to understand what's happening in the world. That doesn't mean 3rd grade teachers should explain high school–level government concepts to their students during election season, but students will be interested in understanding some basics of how the electoral college works. During the 2018 midterm election, one of my students asked what the difference was between the Congress and the Senate. When I explained Congress had two houses—the Senate and the House of Representatives—multiple students demanded to understand how that worked. When these types of questions arise, I try to find age-appropriate articles to read with students in class. Websites like Newsela.com feature articles about history and current events that teachers can adjust for their students' reading levels.

My students also wanted to talk about a lot of controversial topics that adults shy away from: taking a knee during the national anthem, immigration policy, police brutality, climate change, child poverty, and gender discrimination. I insisted on the talk norms discussed previously, despite knowing that adults struggle to use these same norms. I also told the students that I would make sure we had a respectful conversation, and I would ask probing questions to help them explain their thinking or consider another viewpoint. One thing I never did was tell students my opinion. As their teacher, I was there to facilitate the conversation, answer questions when I could, and find resources to help them obtain more information. On occasion, it's impossible to completely conceal a strong opinion, but I make every effort to leave my personal feelings out of the discussion; I emphasize to students that they need to make up their own minds, no matter what an authority figure thinks.

These discussions also make space for students to share their identities and cultures authentically. Too often, teachers attempt to be culturally responsive by essentializing student identities and presenting material that is based on stereotypes, not on actual knowledge of children and their families. For instance, based on last names or physical appearance, teachers may assume students celebrate certain holidays or practice a particular religion. Teachers might also assume that students will not be interested in a particular topic simply because of their appearance. These types of assumptions can lead to uncomfortable, if not biased and exclusionary, learning environments, and frankly, they avoid the much harder work of getting to know the people who make up a classroom community. Through student and family surveys, meetings, phone calls, and day-to-day open conversations, we can find out topics students want to learn more about and discuss. Family surveys can reveal important dates throughout the year, traditions, family sayings, preferred modes of communication, and important values. We can use all these tools to make discussions relevant and highly interesting to our students.

Low-Stakes Activities

Whether the topic is a classroom issue or a current event, teachers can engage students in low-stakes activities to create space for these conversations. During morning meetings or other shared times, we can lead stand up/ sit down debates, where students use their position to show if they agree or disagree with a statement. The class can read an article about a current event for knowledge building to inform a discussion. We can also pose scenarios for students to problem-solve—for instance, by asking, "What should you do when you don't have anyone to play with at recess?" Sometimes a conversation can start with a thought-provoking quote. I would write quotes from Maya Angelou, Albert Einstein, and Frederick Douglass in the classroom morning message and then ask students to explain what they thought about them.

Conclusion

The primary job of an educator is to teach, but the real joy of teaching comes from the cultivation of community. Connection and a sense of belonging are not "extras"; they are the active ingredients that make teachers and their students happy to be together. Such warm, nurturing environments allow for engagement in risk taking and deep thinking. Schools and teachers have an important responsibility in crafting these environments, and the planning requires the same attention to detail as a lesson plan. The work is challenging, but worth it.

Chapter 7 Key Points

- Tell the story of your class by highlighting the behaviors you want to see. Provide an optimistic vision of the future that induces students to buy in.

- Celebrate struggle, and make errors and revisions a normal part of the classroom environment.

- Model intellectual honesty by sharing your own nuanced thoughts with students. Do not be afraid to admit mistakes or publicly account for changing your mind.

- Normalize the existence of multiple perspectives and disagreement by engaging students in dialogue. Talk through norms of debate, respectful disagreement, and an openness to changing your mind.

Further Reading

- *Motivated Teaching: Harnessing the Science of Motivation to Boost Attention and Effort in the Classroom* by Peps Mccrea

- *Troublemakers: Lessons in Freedom from Young Children at School* by Carla Shalaby

CONCLUSION

On my first day of teaching, I neglected to check the weather report. I ignored the gray skies as I led my 2nd graders across the parking lot to the playground. The children ran about while I leaned against the fence and caught my breath. Twenty-two years old, I thought about how tired I was after a long day without a lunch break, or any break at all. I thought about a lot—while ignoring the looming dark clouds above. Once the rain started, I hurried the children into a line and led them across the parking lot to the door. Of course, this is where the real catastrophe began: the door was locked. At this point, the children and I all started screaming and banging on the door. In all honesty, I cannot recall if we waited a few minutes or a half hour, but eventually someone rescued us. The kids all ran ahead of me down the hallway and up the stairs to the classroom. I trailed behind, my drenched shoes squeaking on the floor, begging them to wait.

The lessons of this book can illuminate some of the problems of that day. The stress and demands of teaching had overwhelmed my working memory because I lacked adequate knowledge in my long-term memory. For this reason, I attended to only the surface features of my tasks, so when the schedule said recess, I took my class out for recess. It never occurred to me I would need to account for the weather or check the door. I definitely was *not* thinking critically.

It's been 11 years since that memorable first day. At the time, I thought I had made the biggest mistake of my life. Since that day, I have met so many new teachers who experienced the exact same sense of failure and regret. I hope some are reading this book. We are all, at different points in our career, trapped in the metaphorical rain, unable to open a locked door. My dearest wish for this book is to help some of you crack open that door.

When we as teachers establish our vision and instructional planning, we do the same for students. And giving children time and space to know their own minds in the classroom has never been more important. We live in a time where misinformation and inflammatory rhetoric are everywhere. Children are constantly told, from all angles, what they are supposed to think—as are teachers. Our profession is too often beholden to fads more akin to religious revivals than serious attempts to improve the learning experiences of children.

In school, there are certain nonnegotiable values we share with students: inclusion, care, community mindfulness, hard work. But no matter how hard we try, we cannot presume to think for children. We will not always be with them when they need to decide how to resolve a conflict with a friend or when they decide whether to tell a white lie—and we certainly won't be with them when they're in the voting booth. As teachers, we approach most classroom problems by thinking about how we can control what is happening within the classroom's walls. But the truth is that we cannot control the minds of our children, and it would be quite sad if we tried to. What we can do is provide them with the environment, experiences, and instruction that do something more radical: trust them to learn a lot, think, and then proceed to make their own judgments about the world. I suspect we'll be quite happy with the results.

Before I end, I wish to acknowledge that teaching is an embattled profession, with little trust, unreliable access to support and resources, and ever-changing expectations. To the teachers who experience the unique slings and arrows of this profession and still commit to continuous improvement, your contributions to the children in your community are of immeasurable value. I have often said the person with the most power to effect change in a school is the teacher—there is no administrator who will teach a child to read, or encourage them to think a little more deeply about a question, or support them in revising their work. (I say this as an administrator. To my fellow administrators, your most crucial duty is to foster the environment where teachers can enact great things. Certainly no easy feat!) I opened this book with a call to expand our definition of what is possible for elementary students, but the same expansion applies to elementary educators. This book was written with you, and your capacity for greatness, in mind.

REFERENCES

Abrami, P. C., Bernard, R. M., Borokhovski, E., Waddington, D. I., Wade, C. A., & Persson, T. (2015). Strategies for teaching students to think critically: A meta-analysis. *Review of Educational Research, 85*(2), 275–314. JSTOR. doi:10.3102/0034654314551063

An, S., & Cardona-Maguigad, A. (2019, December 3). *Common Core: Higher expectations, flat results.* WBEZ Chicago, NPR. https://www.npr.org/local/309 /2019/12/03/784224482/common-core-higher-expectations-flat-results

Bloom, B. S. (Ed.). (1956). *Taxonomy of educational objectives: The classification of educational goals: Handbook 1, cognitive domain.* Longman.

Building Learning Power. (n.d.). *Building learning power.* https://www.building learningpower.com/

Chi, M. T. H., & VanLehn, K. A. (2012). Seeing deep structure from the interactions of surface features. *Educational Psychologist, 47*(3), 177–188. doi:10.1080/00461 520.2012.695709

Coyne, M. D., McCoach, D. B., Ware, S., Austin, C. R., Loftus-Rattan, S. M., & Baker, D. L. (2019). Racing against the vocabulary gap: Matthew effects in early vocabulary instruction and intervention. *Exceptional Children, 85*(2), 163–179. doi:10.1177/0014402918789162

Craik, F. I. M., & Lockhart, R. S. (1972). Levels of processing: A framework for memory research. *Journal of Verbal Learning and Verbal Behavior, 11*(6), 671–684. doi:10.1016/S0022-5371(72)80001-X.

Duff, D., Tomblin, J. B., & Catts, H. (2015). The influence of reading on vocabulary growth: A case for a Matthew effect. *Journal of Speech, Language, and Hearing Research, 58*(3), 853–864. doi:10.1044/2015_JSLHR-L-13-0310

Endres, T., & Renkl, A. (2015). Mechanisms behind the testing effect: An empirical investigation of retrieval practice in meaningful learning. *Frontiers in Psychology, 6,* article 1054. doi:10.3389/fpsyg.2015.01054

Facione, P. A. (1990). *Critical thinking: A statement of expert consensus for purposes of educational assessment and instruction: Executive summary: "The Delphi report."* California Academic Press. https://www.qcc.cuny.edu/socialsciences/ppecorino/CT-Expert-Report.pdf

Freireich, A., & Platzer, B. (2021, August 28). The pandemic broke a fundamental principle of teaching. *The Atlantic.* https://www.theatlantic.com/education/archive/2021/08/pandemic-broke-fundamental-principle-teaching/619922/

Frey, P. W., & Adesman, P. (1976). Recall memory for visually presented chess positions. *Memory and Cognition, 4*(5), 541–547. doi:10.3758/BF03213216

Kluger, A. N., & DeNisi, A. (1996). The effects of feedback interventions on performance: A historical review, a meta-analysis, and a preliminary feedback intervention theory. *Psychological Bulletin, 119*(2), 254–284. doi:10.1037/0033-2909.119.2.254

Los Angeles Daily News. (2017, August 28). Common Core will require more critical thinking from students. https://www.dailynews.com/2010/08/02/common-core-will-require-more-critical-thinking-from-students/

Loveless, T. (2015). *The 2015 Brown Center report on American education: How well are American students learning?* Brookings Institution. https://www.brookings.edu/wp-content/uploads/2016/06/2015-Brown-Center-Report_FINAL-3.pdf

Loveless, T. (2022, May 15). *Evidence, struggling math students, and California's 2022 math framework* [Blog post]. Tom Loveless. https://tomloveless.com/posts/evidence-struggling-math-students-and-californias-2022-math-framework/

MacSuga-Gage, A. S., & Simonsen, B. (2015). Examining the effects of teacher-directed opportunities to respond on student outcomes: A systematic review of the literature. *Education and Treatment of Children, 38*(2), 211–239.

Martin, B., Sargent, K., Van Camp, A., & Wright, J. (2018). *Intensive intervention practice guide: Increasing opportunities to respond as an intensive intervention.* U.S. Department of Education, Office of Special Education Programs. http://files.eric.ed.gov/fulltext/ED591076.pdf

National Assessment of Educational Progress. (n.d). *NAEP long-term trend assessment results: Reading and mathematics.* https://www.nationsreportcard.gov/highlights/ltt/2022/

National Governors Association Center for Best Practices, Council of Chief State School Officers. (2010a). *Common Core state standards for English language arts & literacy in history/social studies, science, and technical subjects.* https://learning.ccsso.org/wp-content/uploads/2022/11/ELA_Standards1.pdf

National Governors Association Center for Best Practices, Council of Chief State School Officers. (2010b). *Common Core state standards for mathematics.* https://learning.ccsso.org/wp-content/uploads/2022/11/Math_Standards1.pdf

Nokes-Malach, T. J., VanLehn, K., Belenky, D. M., Lichtenstein, M., & Cox, G. (2013). Coordinating principles and examples through analogy and self-explanation. *European Journal of Psychology of Education, 28,* 1237–1263. doi:10.1007 /s10212-012-0164-z

O'Connor, T. (2021). Emergent properties. In *The Stanford encyclopedia of philosophy.* https://plato.stanford.edu/archives/win2021/entries/properties-emergent/

Organisation for Economic Co-operation and Development. (2016). *PISA 2015 results (Volume II): Policies and practices for successful schools.* PISA, OECD Publishing. https://www.oecd-ilibrary.org/education/pisa-2015-results -volume-ii_9789264267510-en

Organisation for Economic Co-operation and Development. (2019). *PISA 2018 released field trial and main survey new reading items.* https://www.oecd.org /pisa/test/PISA2018_Released_REA_Items_12112019.pdf

Oxford English Dictionary. (n.d.). Critical thinking. *OED.com.* Retrieved April 14, 2022, from https://www.oed.com/view/Entry/44592

Ramaprasad, A. (1983). On the definition of feedback. *Behavioral Science, 28*(1), 4–13. doi:10.1002/bs.3830280103

Reed, S. K., Dempster, A., & Ettinger, M. (1985). Usefulness of analogous solutions for solving algebra word problems. *Journal of Experimental Psychology: Learning, Memory, and Cognition, 11*(1), 106–125. doi:10.1037/0278-7393 .11.1.106

Richey, J. E., & Nokes-Malach, T. J. (2015). Comparing four instructional techniques for promoting robust knowledge. *Educational Psychology Review, 27,* 181–218. doi:10.1007/s10648-014-9268-0

Rittle-Johnson, B. (2006). Promoting transfer: Effects of self-explanation and direct instruction. *Child Development, 77*(1), 1–15. https://www.jstor.org /stable/3696686

Rittle-Johnson, B., Schneider, M., & Star, J. R. (2015). Not a one-way street: Bidirectional relations between procedural and conceptual knowledge of mathematics. *Educational Psychology Review, 27,* 587–597. doi:10.1007 s10648-015-9302-x

Roediger, H. L., III, Putnam, A. L., & Smith, M. A. (2011). Chapter one—Ten benefits of testing and their applications to educational practice. *Psychology of Learning and Motivation, 55,* 1–36. doi:10.1016/B978-0-12-387691-1.00001-6

Rosenshine, B. (2010). *Principles of instruction.* (Educational Practices Series-21). UNESCO International Bureau of Education. http://www.ibe.unesco.org/file admin/user_upload/Publications/Educational_Practices/EdPractices_21.pdf

Rumelhart, D. E. (1981). Schemata: The building blocks of cognition. In J. T. Guthrie (Ed.), *Comprehension and teaching: Research reviews* (pp. 3–26). International Reading Association.

Russell, B. (1916, June). Education as a political institution. *The Atlantic.* https:// .theatlantic.com/magazine/archive/1916/06/education-as-a-political-institution/ 305258/

Russo, J., & Hopkins, S. (2019). Teachers' perceptions of students when observing lessons involving challenging tasks. *International Journal of Science and Mathematics Education, 17,* 759–779. doi:10.1007/s10763-018-9888-9

Sherrington, T. (2021, October 30). *Weaving it all together: 9 key threads for maximising learning.* Teacherhead. https://teacherhead.com/2021/10/30 /weaving-it-all-together-9-key-threads-for-maximising-learning/

Siegler, R. S. (1994). Cognitive variability: A key to understanding cognitive development. *Current Directions in Psychological Science, 3*(1), 1–5.

Smith, R., Snow, P., Serry, T., & Hammond, L. (2021). The role of background knowledge in reading comprehension: A critical review. *Reading Psychology, 42*(3), 214–240. doi:10.1080/02702711.2021.1888348

Stanovich, K. E. (1986). Matthew effects in reading: Some consequences of individual differences in the acquisition of literacy. *Reading Research Quarterly, 21*(4), 360–407.

Steinbeck, J. (2002).... Like captured fireflies. *America and Americans, and selected nonfiction* (S. Shillinglaw & J. J. Benson, Eds.). Viking.

Sweller, J. (2016). Working memory, long-term memory, and instructional design. *Journal of Applied Research in Memory and Cognition, 5*(4), 360–367. doi:10 .1016/j.jarmac.2015.12.002

Willingham, D. T. (2003, Summer). Ask the cognitive scientist: Students remember... what they think about. *American Educator.* https://www.aft./periodical /american-educator/summer-2003/ask-cognitive-scientist-students-rememberwhat-they-think

Willingham, D. (2007, Summer). Critical thinking: Why is it so hard to teach? *American Educator,* 8–19. https://www.aft.org/sites/default/files/media/2014 /Crit_Thinking.pdf

Willingham, D. T. (2008, Summer). Ask the cognitive scientist: What is developmentally appropriate practice? *American Educator,* 34–39. https://www.aft.org/sites /default/files/media/2014/willingham_1.pdf

Willingham, D. T. (2009). *Why don't students like school? A cognitive scientist answers questions about how the mind works and what it means for the classroom.* Jossey-Bass.

Willingham, D. T. (2020, Fall). Ask the cognitive scientist: How can educators teach critical thinking? *American Educator.* https://www.aft.org/ae/fall2020 /willingham

INDEX

The letter *f* following a page locator denotes a figure.

ABOUT THE AUTHOR

 **Erin Shadowens** believes in the power of school communities to provide children with rich and robust educational experiences. She spent 10 years teaching every grade from kindergarten to 3rd, discovering in that time that every child, no matter how young, is capable of taking on academic challenges. Her classroom work was recognized with the 2020 Excellence in Teaching Award from Learning for Justice (formerly Teaching Tolerance). After 10 years in the classroom, Erin moved into a school leadership role. She now serves as the Director of Lower School at Brooklyn Prospect Downtown Elementary. More of Erin's education-related writing is available at https://preptime.substack.com.

Related ASCD Resources: Instructional Strategies

At the time of publication, the following resources were available (ASCD stock numbers in parentheses).

Books

Demystifying Discussion: How to Teach and Assess Academic Conversation Skills, K–5 by Jennifer Orr (#122003)

Nurturing Habits of Mind in Early Childhood: Success Stories from Classrooms Around the World edited by Arthur L. Costa and Bena Kallick (#119017)

Project Based Teaching: How to Create Rigorous and Engaging Learning Experiences by Suzie Boss and John Larmer (#118047)

Rigor by Design, Not Chance: Deeper Thinking Through Actionable Instruction and Assessment by Karin Hess (#122036)

Teaching for Deeper Learning: Tools to Engage Students in Meaning Making by Jay McTighe and Harvey F. Silver (#120022)

Quick Reference Guides

Cultivating Habits of Mind by Arthur L. Costa and Bena Kallick (#QRG117098)

The Formative Assessment Learning Cycle (Quick Reference Guide) by Susan M. Brookhart and Jay McTighe (#QRG117085)

Giving Students Effective Feedback (Quick Reference Guide) by Susan M. Brookhart (#QRG116087)

Improving Classroom Discussion by Jackie Acree Walsh (#QRG117053)

Increasing Rigor in the Classroom by Barbara Blackburn (#QRG119044)

For up-to-date information about ASCD resources, go to www.ascd.org. You can search the complete archives of *Educational Leadership* at www.ascd.org /el. To contact us, send an email to member@ascd.org or call 1-800-933-2723 or 703-578-9600.

WHOLE CHILD
TENETS

ascd
whole child

The ASCD Whole Child approach is an effort to transition from a focus on narrowly defined academic achievement to one that promotes the long-term development and success of all children. Through this approach, ASCD supports educators, families, community members, and policymakers as they move from a vision about educating the whole child to sustainable, collaborative actions.

Critical Thinking in the Elementary Classroom relates to the **engaged, supported,** and **challenged** tenets. *For more about the ASCD Whole Child approach, visit* ***www.ascd.org /wholechild.***

1 HEALTHY
Each student enters school healthy and learns about and practices a healthy lifestyle.

2 SAFE
Each student learns in an environment that is physically and emotionally safe for students and adults.

3 ENGAGED
Each student is actively engaged in learning and is connected to the school and broader community.

4 SUPPORTED
Each student has access to personalized learning and is supported by qualified, caring adults.

5 CHALLENGED
Each student is challenged academically and prepared for success in college or further study and for employment and participation in a global environment.

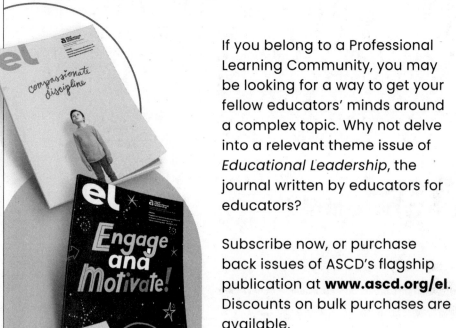